THE

The Cancer Cure Diet for Dogs

The Dogington Post

The Cancer Cure Diet for Dogs
by The Dogington Post
with Foreword by Dr. Harlan Kilstein and Lori R. Taylor

Copyright © 2018 by Woof Publishing Inc.
All rights reserved.

ISBN-13: 978-0692974018 (Woof Publishing Corp)

The information in this book is not intended as medical diagnosis and should not replace your dog's veterinary care.

While the author has made every effort to provide accurate Internet addresses at the time of publication, neither the publisher nor the author assumes any responsibility for errors or changes that occur after publication. Further, the publisher does not have control over and does not assume responsibility for author or third-party websites or their content.

www.dogingtonpost.com

To Molly & Virgil.
Forever in our hearts.

Foreword

If humans were dying from cancer at the same rate as dogs it would be a national emergency.

Politicians would be campaigning about getting more money for research.

The cost of all treatments would be covered by insurance.

But instead of talking about humans, we are talking about man's best friend. And the numbers are shocking.

Somewhere around 40% of all dogs will die from cancer. And all we hear is crickets.

When I adopted a ketogenic diet I started noticing that it has had great success with fighting cancer in humans. In fact, more and more books and studies are reporting amazing results in treating cancer with nutrition.

Once again, when it comes to dogs, we hear nothing.

Then, a shining light on the horizon – the Keto Pet Sanctuary began taking in dogs with cancer, curing them with a Ketogenic diet, and finding forever homes for these dogs.

We knew that we had the potential to bring a cure for cancer to millions of dog owners – starting with you.

You will learn exactly who the real culprits are and a step-by-step process for slowing, stopping, sometimes even reversing the disease.

We hope this book helps your fur kid.

We'd like to dedicate the book to the following groups:

To all the veterinarians who put their heart and soul into helping our dogs deal with cancer.

To all the dog owners who never give up on their fur babies until their final breath.

To all the dogs who have crossed the Rainbow Bridge because of cancer.

I'd like to salute two individuals whose lives revolve around their love of animals:

Brandy Arnold, Editor of the The Dogington Post and Brooke Arnold, Editor of the The Catington Post.

And to our incredible author, Jill Stevens for putting her heart and soul into this book.

Please let us know if this book makes an impact on your fur kids.

Harlan D. Kilstein Ed.D.
Publisher, The Dogington Post
topdog@dogingtonpost.com

"Lori, I have terrible news, Truman has cancer"

So many questions raced through my mind…

How could this have happened? Was it something I did? How does a healthy, young dog suddenly develop cancer?

And more importantly…now what?

After hundreds of hours of diligently researching the topic of true optimal nutrition for dogs, I stumbled across a shocking study by Texas A & M stating that your dog is 4 times more likely to die from breast cancer, 8 times more likely to die from bone cancer and 32 times more likely to die of skin cancer.

Skin cancer, I thought?

They have fur!

What was going on?

And that's the day I became a maniac on a mission, feverishly searching for solutions for the best way to feed our fur babies. Sadly, it didn't take that long to quickly discover most bags of food had nothing to do with what dogs would eat in the wild. It was all about convenience and I was horrified to realize just how much I didn't know.

And while I can't prove kibble was the catalyst for Truman's cancer, there was no doubt a better way. After years of consulting with the best veterinarians America has to offer, my team developed the most natural way to feed our dogs we could: easy-to-feed raw dog foods, treats, supplements and chews created to give pet parents better, life-saving, options. We created what I consider to be one of the premiere and most robust nutrition systems on the planet, and our pet parent's results couldn't be more inspiring.

Here's just one of many heartfelt messages I get from pet parents every day. This one is from Arlene L. in New York:

> *"I originally ordered the Boost Me on a promotion. I figured if my dog doesn't like it, I won't be out a lot of money. I also ordered because I read the info about this product. My Boston Terrier had these fairly large growths on her neck and side. The vet told me that they had cancerous cells in them and wanted me to have them removed. Long story short, the growth on her neck completely disappeared within a month of feeding her Boost Me, Feed Me, and Treat Me. I only added these in addition to her regular food. I scheduled surgery to have the tumor on her side removed. About a month after the first growth disappeared, the other one went down dramatically. I cancelled the surgery and opted to keep a eye on it. I can't say 100% that it was your foods and treats that did it, but that's the only thing I changed in her routine. In my opinion, I feel that they have helped her in a big way. At 9 years old, lately she has more pep and energy than ever before.*

Sometimes she even acts like a puppy. Both her and my other dog love it. They chow down on their food now like it's the greatest thing in the world. If my dogs love to eat their food with Boost Me, along with your other products, and they positively benefit my babies, then I'm sold!"

Arlene's story is a perfect example of how proper nutrition can combat canine cancer, even after it's formed. We don't have to settle for poor health and early deaths in our fur babies. So while, again, I can't prove the food is what made the difference, I do get to look at myself in the mirror and know I'm doing everything I can to stack the deck in my dog's favor.

Armed with the knowledge in this book, you too, can take measures to do the best you can by your dog. Like everything else in life, no matter how well you think you're doing, there's always a way to do better…

And after all our dogs do for us, aren't they worthy of "better?"

Love Your Dog's Life,
Lori R. Taylor
Founder, TruPet LLC

CONTENTS

Why Does It Seem Like Less Food?
What if My Dog Is Hungry on the Ketogenic Diet?
Tips For When You Canine Does Want To Eat

INTRODUCTION

Love at first sight.

If you're reading these words, you've most likely experienced it. That knowing. That connection. That deep understanding that comes when you meet your potential-new-family-member for the very first time.

Whether at a shelter, first pick of the litter or even a pet store window (we'll come back to that issue in another book!), you know when you see him or her for the very first time that it's meant to be. That you two belong together.

This is simply how it is for dog owners.

It's puppy love...even if your new best friend is an adult when you first meet.

I get it. Your deep, unconditional love for your dog knows no bounds. That four-legged ball of fluff or short-haired jumper or elegant creature standing at attention becomes your constant companion.

And this is the book that no loving dog owner wants to pick up let alone read, but it could save your canine companion's life. Because let's face it. Cancer kills. It doesn't have to, but right now, the numbers of cancer-related deaths in our four-legged community, are astronomically high.

Yet, you can do something about it. Whether you have a cancer diagnosis or want to prevent one, this book is going to show you exactly how to help your four-legged best friend.

See, your dog depends on you, looks up to you and trusts you to provide, not just for its basic needs of food and water, but everything. Your dog wants direction from you - even if half the time he doesn't really listen.

Your dog wants unconditional love from you and will go to any lengths to please you. With fun moments like creating a disaster area in the middle of your freshly made bed, or destroying your favorite chair - your dog is always there, tail wagging, ready to "help."

Your dog wants to comfort you when you're down.

Your dog is always ready for what you want and is willing to walk excitedly, eyes glued to your every move when you're on the go.

Your dog tells you all it can by following you everywhere, barking, and by wagging its long tail or short stump (yes, wiggle butts, I'm referring to you!).

If you really want to be entertained, go to YouTube and search for talking dogs video. It cheers up even the saddest of souls.

(Don't tell me you've never indulged!)

Yet, there are some things your dog may hide from you, and no, it's not just their favorite bone in the sofa cushions. Let's face it, when our precious, best friends are in pain, they usually choose to hide it from us.

Yes, we have movies like the 1955 Walt Disney classic *Lady And The Tramp*, (love that string of spaghetti), cartoons, and TV shows, like a more current ABC Comedy, *Downward Dog*, that brings anthropomorphism to an entirely new, clever and funny level. However, the reality is your dog can't stand up on their hind legs, wave a paw to get your attention and literally say, "Hey Mom (or Dad), I'm in pain."

And that's the hardest part…you don't know what you don't know, until it's too late!

For example, did you know up to 60% of domesticated dogs in the United States of America alone are diagnosed with cancer in their lifetime? And up to 40% of our beloved canine friends, who are given a cancer diagnosis, actually die from cancer.

Those are staggeringly high numbers. Sadly, you may be aware of these stats as you've already fallen victim to them, (more on how we can help support you, in just a moment).

First, let's put that number into perspective...

Say you're at your local dog park playing fetch with your four-legged friend. You might be there with some of your other doggy-loving-friends, who've also brought their besties.

If you look around and see nine other dogs in that park, as your dog chases after the ball you've just thrown for him - again, you can bet that with 99% certainty that four out of those dogs (ten in total) will experience the big C word in their lifetime.

And yes, the C word is cancer.

And as one year equals seven dog years for our four-legged-friends, due to their faster metabolic rate, that diagnosis won't necessarily be toward the end of their time on this earth.

In fact, veterinarians see an alarming increase in early-age cancer in dogs, that yes, by all rights should scare you. It scares me.

But don't worry.

You are reading this Dogington Post sponsored book for a reason.

You love your four-legged best friend. You either have a cancer diagnosis for your dog or you want to know what to do in the event you and your canine friend are hit with the news in the coming years. Or, you want to take preventative steps now so your faithful companion can live a long and healthy life, cancer-free.

Well, my dog-loving friend, you are in the right place and here's why:

I have a dog. I love my dog. I'd do anything - A.N.Y.T.H.I.N.G - for my furry friend. And I have, to the tune of thousands of dollars in vet bills.

See, your vet wants to help you.

Your veterinarian probably got into the profession for his or her own love of dogs (or gasp, cats!) but they are often restricted. Veterinarians are bound by known, proven science, restricted by regulations, and, are very, highly compensated for the items they sell, such as food, which studies have shown might just be causing the health problems in our dogs in the first place! (GASP)

Our motivation is simple. We love dogs. We want our own dogs to be healthy, active, playful and live long lives.

And we want the same for you and your bestie. So we've done something insane.

We've researched…
• What Causes Dog Cancer
• What Cures Dog Cancer
• Why This Works
• How This Works

…And found stories that prove that what you will read in the coming pages works.

But here's the thing, you don't have to read this book from start to finish, from page one to the end.

See, we've broken this book down into some easy to reference sections so you can immediately go to the area you need to best suit your current situation.

Why? Because we know you might be facing a cancer diagnosis for your best friend right right now, and you might be overwhelmed right now. We get it. And we want to get you right to where you need to be fast.

If you currently have a dog with a cancer diagnosis, turn to Chapter 13:

"What To Do When You Get A C-Diagnosis From Your Vet"

If you have a desire to understand this not-so-new diet that can help your four-legged friend, you'll want to dive into the sections on

"Healthier Dogs - The Keto Way"

If you want to go into a deeper study of all this, turn to these two sections:

"Understanding the C-Word at a Basic Level" in Chapter 1 and
"Signs The Ketogenic Diet is Working" in Chapter 6

If you just what to know what to feed your four-legged friend for best health right now, turn to the sections

"Bottom Line: What Do I Feed My Dog On the Keto Diet?" in Chapter 3
"Shopping the Keto Way" in Chapter 8
"Preparing Your Canine's Ketogenic Diet - Simplified" in Chapter 9

Then read up on Chapter 1:

"What Is The Ketogenic Diet For Dogs"
"How the Keto Diet Works for Dogs"
"What Does the Keto Diet For Dogs Look Like?"

And these sections:

"Introducing Your Dog to Keto the Easy Way" in Chapter 2
"The Math Behind the Ketogenic Diet - Made Easy" in Chapter 4
"Four Examples of the Keto Diet - Calculated" in Chapter 5

If you want some proof that this works, check out:

"Doggy Success Tales" in Chapter 7
"Success Stories of Pets on the Ketogenic Diet" in Chapter 17

While there are more sections, and a full break down can be found in the table of contents at the front of this guide, we've made this book an informative, easy-to-read reference manual that you can refer back to again and again as needed.

Why?

Because we care.

Because we want to see those C-diagnosis in our beloved doggy friends' numbers drop drastically.

Because they can drop. Because dogs with cancer should not become the norm. Because, with a little bit of knowledge, we can help heal our four-legged, best friends and enjoy their loyalty, love, and companionship for as long as possible.

Your dog relies on you for everything. Let me repeat that.

Your dog relies on YOU for E.V.E.R.Y.T.H.I.N.G.

And that's a lot of pressure, especially when you have a sick dog to care for. Now you can rely on us to help you find answers.

Turn the page and discover exactly what you need to know, exactly what to do and exactly how to do it, as easily as possible, so that you can help your dog, possibly heal your dog, while saving hundreds, if not thousands, of dollars in vet bills that come with no guarantee.

Don't wait for the horrible cancer diagnosis. Get educated now.

And if you're already in the nightmare of a cancer diagnosis, you are in the right place, so breathe easy and dive into the section that matters most to you at this moment.

We are here for you and the health of your canine friend.

We are a group of dedicated pet parents who run an online website called The Dogington Post. We are pet-owners first, who love our dogs and don't want to see cancer take any more furry lives.

We simply love dogs. Some of us have lost canines to cancer, so this book is personal. Some of us are going through the battle of fighting cancer with our four-legged friend right now. So this book is very personal.

And some of us are into prevention through nutrition, so our canine's - yours and mine - can stay active, healthy, happy and cancer free.

This is who we are and why we are here for you and your four-legged best friend.

The Cancer Cure
Diet for Dogs

CHAPTER 1:
The Diet That Saves Dogs' Lives

The American Cancer Society estimates that each year approximately six million dogs, in the United States alone, are given a cancer diagnosis. Imagine that number when combined with other countries.

I don't know about you, but I'm shocked by it.

First, that the American Cancer Society is even tracking cancer in our four-legged canine friends because it's that widespread.

And second, that because they are tracking numbers, it must be on the rise and becoming more and more of an epidemic.

But, friend, this frightening number of cancer diagnosis should be our wake-up call to say we are simply doing something wrong when it comes to our animals.

Before we move on, I'd like us to agree on something relatively simple.

The food we feed our animals, especially our dogs, is not natural.

Nowhere in the history of canines were dogs raised on "cereal" or grains, as they are today.

In order to dive into the next section, we must first agree that whether in people or our beloved animals, there is a connection between the food we eat and the appearance of cancer.

See, cancer cells are simply unhealthy cells, and science has begun to show that when these deformed cancer cells are starved, they stop growing and in some cases, these cells shrink and at times, disappear altogether.

So our dogs, eating a diet, which is high in carbs, when we know for a fact that carbs become sugar and sugar feeds cancer…well, we are creating a perfect storm of an environment for this devastating disease to wreak havoc in our canine (and other animal) friends.

With the basic understanding that we are what we eat… let's dive into a now popular diet which in fact dates back to ancient times.

It's called the Ketogenic Diet, and it's not just for the dogs!

SUMMARY
In this section you discovered

- Approximately six million dogs, in the United States alone, are given a cancer diagnosis each year.
- The food we feed our animals, especially our dogs, is not natural.
- Dogs were never meant to be raised on "cereal" or grains, as they are today.
- At no time in history, have dogs naturally eaten cereal for any meal on any day.
- There is a connection between the food we eat and the appearance of cancer.
- Cancer cells are simply unhealthy cells.
- We are creating a perfect storm of an environment for cancer to wreak havoc in our canine (and other animal) friends because we are simply not educated enough. And that stops here!

A More Familiar Name for the Ketogenic Diet
First, let's give the Ketogenic Diet a name you might be slightly more familiar with if you ever wanted to shed a few pounds in the last, gosh, forty years, or knew someone who did.

Ever heard of Dr. Atkins, or the Atkin's Diet, a widely popular way to fight obesity by minimizing the consumption of carbs and focusing on protein?

Well, Dr. Robert C. Atkins, a cardiologist created his tri-level diet plan and messaging based on the Ketogenic Diet, which has been around since ancient times.

Imagine that.

The Ketogenic Diet has been used to help numerous conditions over the last one hundred years and has steadily gained in popularity.

The History of the Ketogenic Diet - Demystified!
See another Doctor, R.M. Wilder, was the one to first develop the Ketogenic Diet as a way to mimic or imitate the effects that other

treatments were having on human cancer patients.

It was Dr. R.M. Wilder, back in 1921, a physician from the Mayo Clinic in Minnesota, who gave the Keto Diet, short for Ketogenic, it's name.

Dr. Wilder theorized that the metabolic state of fasting could be maintained long-term with a Ketogenic Diet because this way of eating mimicked starvation by limiting carbohydrates and providing high amounts of dietary fat.

Now, when a person fasts, the cells, both good cells and unhealthy cancer cells, are starved.

A very good thing for unhealthy cells, and as it turns out, and not a new theory, as this was first brought to light by Otto Warburg, a German biochemist, but widely dismissed at the time.

Like many new science-based discoveries that aren't clearly understood, Warburg's idea of starving cancer cells was dismissed for decades - until now. We'll come back to Warburg, the biochemist, in just a bit.

But with Dr. R.M. Wilder's results, fasting became a way to minimize a cancer patient's condition.

However, the stress of fasting on the human body was severe, especially given a body riddled with cancer, so Dr. R.M. Wilder used his research into the Keto Diet to develop a similar reaction within the human body.

The Keto Diet created a biochemical reaction within the human body, back in the early 1920s, that was similar to what happened when a patient fasted.

And the Keto Diet worked for cancer patients as far back as the early 1920s!

Why the Keto Diet Worked in the 1920s

The body uses fat from the Keto Diet and remains in a state of "ketosis" as long as the diet is strictly maintained. Ketosis is a natural process the body initiates to help us survive when food intake is low.

SUMMARY
In this section you discovered
- When a person fasts, the cells, both good cells and unhealthy cancer cells, are starved.
- Dr. Wilder theorized that the metabolic state of fasting could be maintained long-term with a Ketogenic Diet.
- This way of eating mimicked starvation, by limiting carbohydrates and providing high amounts of dietary fat.
- Fasting became a way to minimize a cancer patient's condition.
- The Ketogenic Diet worked for cancer patients as far back as the early 1920s!

What Science Is Saying About the Ketogenic Diet
In the last thirty years, that research, using the Keto Diet to fight cancer in humans, was put to the test with animals given the same diagnosis.

And again, it worked.

The effects of the diet were positive and cancerous tumor growth was shown to decrease in most animal patients.

Plus, there was a spike in survival rates for those animals treated using the Keto Diet, who'd been previously diagnosed with various types of cancer.

The Ketogenic Diet For Dogs - In Action
Before we dive into the specifics of the Keto Diet for Dogs, let's meet Dr. Judy Morgan, who has a blog and writes about the custom-tailored-ketogenic-diet she created to combat her dog's needs.

Myra is Dr. Judy Morgan's dog, and she suffers from severe allergies along with lymphoma, a type of cancer that attacks the immune system. Dr. Morgan's main goal for her canine bestie, through a Keto dietary plan, was to starve the cancer cells and provide adequate nutrition for Myra. The base of Myra's diet is simple - nutrient-dense proteins and fats with the absence of carbs or doggy cereal, which is the typical American canine diet.

Now, Myra's owner is a doctor. However, you do not have to be one to place your dog on a Ketogenic Diet. You simply have to love your dog. And I'm going to assume right now that you do.

Like Charlie's owner, who considered him part of the family and like any family member, she was willing to search far and wide to care for him in every way possible. In 2011, Charlie, a 20-pound Bichon-Frise, showed classic signs of cancer, starting with the loss of his appetite.

His diagnosis was a large cancerous mass, requiring surgery, with his chances of surviving the procedure slim. Well, Charlie was a fighter and pulled through surgery. And Charlie's owner committed to putting all efforts into his recovery including switching his diet to fats, proteins and some veggies. The Keto way.

See, I know if you are reading this now, you are very much like Charlie's owner, willing to go the distance to care for your beloved best friend. And even when all hope is lost, there can still be a silver lining found, as proven by the KetoPet Sanctuary, a non-profit organization dedicated to taking on the responsibility to provide for animals given a so-called "incurable" cancer diagnosis.

KetoPet Sanctuary (KPS) stands apart as a leading facility in curing terminal cancer for animals whose owners were told all hope was lost.

For nearly three years (at the time of this publication), this amazing facility has been combating these incurable cases with one weapon - the Ketogenic Diet.

Rob Penna is the co-founder of the KPS facility, and he credits nutrition with being at the core of the reversal of cancer symptoms. He believes that the proper dietary structure can be significantly more effective than the average cancer-treatment drug and has results to prove his claim.

KPS has managed, through a structured Keto Diet, to halt the effects of various cancers in canines brought to the facility with a terminal diagnosis, as well as, in some cases, reverse the conditions altogether.

Cali, a four-and-a-half-year-old Vizsla, is just one example of the many dogs who have successfully recovered from cancer, thanks to the work of the veterinarians and caregivers at the KetoPet Sanctuary.

See, Cali was pregnant when she arrived at the sanctuary and suffering from hemangiosarcoma, in the form of a life-threatening tumor, and in just a few months at the KPS facility, on a Keto Diet, was cancer free.

Did you catch that? In just a few months, Cali was cancer free!

Now, to be clear the KetoPet Sanctuary (KPS) is not against, nor do they deny other forms of cancer treatment, they simply take treatment a step beyond testing, surgery, and drugs. They take treatment to its core by focusing on the canine's diet. KPS goes back to the basics, back to nutrition, to see what can work in each case, such as Cali's, and their success rate is phenomenal.

This Texas-based facility is known for providing treatment for our canine "lost-cause-cases" that is fit for human's, which is providing groundbreaking innovations in the search for a cure.

A cure for our four-legged friends. A cure for our two-legged ones, as well.

KetoPet Sanctuary, a place run by veterinarians and part of the Epigenix Foundation, is quick to share that nutrition and diet are critical to the health of any animal, even for those not suffering from the devastating effects of cancer.

So, let's dive into a good place to start for prevention and proper health of our four-legged friends, and even, their human counterparts.

But first, we must agree with the following statement.

Canines are carnivores.

"Any discussion of canine nutrition needs to start with one basic premise. Dogs, all dogs, even Boston Terriers, are carnivores, not omnivores. The assumption that dogs are omnivores remains to be proven, whereas the truth about dogs being carnivores is very well-supported by the evidence

available to us - [their teeth]." - Dr. Jeannie Thomason
http://www.thewholedog.org/nutrition.html

SUMMARY
In this section, you learned
- KetoPet Sanctuary, a non-profit organization, is dedicated to taking on the responsibility to provide for animals given a so-called "incurable" cancer diagnosis.
- KetoPet Sanctuary (KPS) stands apart as a leading facility in curing terminal cancer for animals whose owners were told all hope was lost.
- KPS takes treatment to its core by focusing on the canine's diet and goes back to the basics, back to nutrition, to see what can work in each case.
- KPS is quick to share that nutrition and diet are critical to the health of any animal, even for those not suffering from the devastating effects of cancer.
- Canines are carnivores.

The Benefits of the Keto Diet - Simply Stated
Let's face it, without proper nutrition in humans, and our besties, every virus, every allergen, every parasite, every bacterium, and every fungus is made all the more pervasive, powerful, and dangerous.

Including cancer, as the rising numbers in our doggy population continue to show. The danger lies not because viruses, allergens, parasites, bacterium, fungus and even cancer are strengthened in any way, but because the body's ability to fight them off is dramatically suppressed.

We see this in our human population today with increased risks of disease and super viruses. One way to look at these super viruses and increased numbers of disease is to instead focus on the body and the break down of the human immune system.

That breakdown can be traced back to one thing - poor nutrition. And the same can be said for our four-legged friends. The natural defense against all these things, the dog's own natural immune system, is dependent on proper nutrition to maintain adequate protection against invasion.

With proper nutrition alone, there is a huge decrease in the need for things like antibiotics, vaccines, and parasiticides. In our canines, and even in ourselves. And proper nutrition starts at home, with you.

The first step is to say goodbye to store bought dry and wet dog food. Then say hello to a new way of living. *The Keto way.* And while it might take some getting used to, the results will simply blow you away.

And who knows, maybe you'll even join your canine on the Keto path and become a fat-burning machine too!

SUMMARY

In this section you discovered
- A dog's own immune system, which is dependent on proper nutrition to maintain adequate protection against invasion, is its best, natural defense against disease.
- With proper nutrition alone, there is a huge decrease in the need for things like antibiotics, vaccines, and parasiticides.
- The first step is to say goodbye to store bought dry and wet dog food.

Understanding Cancer at a Basic Level

But first, back to cancer and a quick rundown of just how this horrid disease functions at a basic level.

Because with understanding comes knowledge. And with knowledge comes power. The power to protect, the power to help, the power to heal your canine friend - and even yourself.

Understanding How Cancer Grows

Remember that biochemist, Otto Warburg, mentioned earlier? Warburg was the German scientist who, in the early 20th century, believed tumors could be treated by disrupting their source of energy, but his ideas were dismissed. See for him, it all started with a sea urchin.

The sea urchin needed tons of oxygen to grow, so in 1923, when Warburg looked at a rat with a cancerous tumor, he expected to see the same thing - a massive consumption of oxygen as the tumor grew. But instead, Warburg saw the cancer cells fueled their growth by swallowing up enormous amounts of glucose (blood sugar) and, even more shocking, were able to break it down without oxygen.

For Warburg, this made no sense because oxygen-fueled reactions are a much more efficient way of turning food into energy. Plus, there was plenty of oxygen for the cancer cells to use to grow. But the cancer cells didn't need the oxygen.

When Warburg tested additional tumors, including ones from humans, he documented the same results every time. The cancerous cells were ravenous for glucose.

That is worth repeating.

Back in 1923, Otto Warburg proved that sugar - glucose - is what cancerous cells thrive on and is what they need to grow.

Today, the Warburg Effect is used to detect up to 80% of cancerous cells in humans through the device known as a PET scan. This scan works simply by revealing the places in the body where cells are consuming extra glucose. The more glucose consumption the PET scan detects typically means a worse C-diagnosis for the patient.

That said, Warburg's discovery proves that cancer is not just an abnormal chromosomes (a mutation of cells passed down genetically) disease, but also a diseased based on nutrients and diet.

And this is good news.

It's good news for you and your canine friend because starting today; you can take control of what your four-legged bestie eats. And if you're super courageous and want to live the best life possible with your canine, you too can do the same.

SUMMARY
In this section you uncovered
- Warburg, a German scientist, believed tumors could be treated by disrupting their source of energy.
- Warburg's ideas were widely dismissed at the time.

- Warburg saw the cancer cells fueled their growth by swallowing up enormous amounts of glucose (blood sugar) and the cells were able to break it down without oxygen.
- Cancer cells didn't need the oxygen.
- Cancer cells thrived on glucose - sugar.
- The Warburg Effect is used to detect up to 80% of cancerous cells in humans through the device known as a PET scan.
- The PET scan works by revealing the places in the body where cells are consuming extra glucose.
- Because we know that cancer thrives on glucose, this knowledge is a powerful indicator of cancerous cells.

What is the Ketogenic Diet for Dogs?

Let's first dive into what the Keto Diet is in general and what it is for dogs.

And if you are interested in going Keto yourself, know there are resources right here in this book to help you maneuver the Keto Diet for your health and well-being as well.

The basic idea of the Ketogenic Diet (or Keto for short) is the following.

A Keto Diet is well known for being a low carb diet, where the body produces ketones in the liver to be used as energy. Ketones-what?!

Ketones are simply a fuel source for the body and the brain much like glucose (or sugar) is a fuel source. See, ketosis is a natural process the body initiates to help us survive when food intake is low. During this state, we produce ketones, which are produced from the breakdown of fats in the liver. The end goal of a properly maintained Keto Diet is to force your body into this metabolic state. This isn't done through starvation of calories but starvation of carbohydrates.

Beyond just providing the brain with fuel, ketones appear to have many therapeutic effects on neurons and are being intensely researched in their applications for epilepsy, Parkinson's, Alzheimer's, depression, anxiety and other neurological disorders in the human population.

The benefits of the Keto Diet are immense, and like most good things in life, require a bit of knowledge and dedication to make them work. Let's dive into how to make the Keto Diet work for your four-legged friend.

SUMMARY
In this section you discovered
- A Keto Diet is well known for being a low carb diet, where the body produces ketones in the liver to be used as energy.
- Ketones are simply a fuel source for the body and the brain much like glucose (or sugar) is a fuel source.
- Ketosis is a natural process the body initiates to help us survive when food intake is low.
- The end goal of a properly maintained Keto Diet is to force your body into this metabolic state.
- Armed with knowledge and dedication, you can make the Ketogenic Diet work for you and your canine.

How the Keto Diet Works for Dogs
You may remember from the last section that a Ketogenic Diet is a low carb, high-fat diet that turns your body (or your canine's body) into a fat-burning machine.

Most people, and due to diet, most of our pets, are on a rollercoaster ride of a sugar-burning diet, not fat-burning one.

Here's the lowdown on how Keto works in the human and doggy body.

Keto, the diet, restricts your intake of sugar and starchy foods, like pasta and bread for humans, and fillers, like sweet potatoes, corn and wheat found in store-bought dog food. When it comes to dog food, it's a huge misunderstanding that "Grain Free" is the same thing as "Carb free." But, that's impossible with kibble due to the high heat process used to make it. It requires a starch to bind it together. For many grain-free kibbles, peas are the "new grains."

Instead, on Keto, you or your bestie will eat delicious, real food with selective protein, healthy fats, and vegetables for nutrients. In some cases, where cancer exists, carbs are all but non-existent on the Keto Diet.

In this book, we will dive into what to eat, what to avoid, and exactly how to do it. But first, a bit more on how the Ketogenic Diet works, because it's important to understand what will happen to your canine friend during this process of a diet change, should you decide to partake and go Keto.

A Ketogenic Diet is designed to induce nutritional ketosis as a metabolic intervention against cancer when combined with daily exercise and standard veterinary care. What?!?

Yep, that sentence got me too, so let's break it down and make it dog-friendly.

NUTRITIONAL KETOSIS DEFINED:

Nutritional Ketosis is a state of health in which your body is efficiently burning fat as its primary fuel source instead of glucose. When undergoing a Ketogenic Diet, you are essentially converting yourself from a "sugar burner" to a "fat burner."

Now, remember Otto Warburg. He's the biochemist who saw that cancer cells thrived on sugar, also known as, glucose.

Smart dude.

Well, when just like he did back in 1923 when we remove what feeds cancer in the human or doggy body - sugar - we've created a metabolic intervention or simply put, a change in the environment inside the body that those pesky cancer cells no longer like. If cancer cells want the sugar to grow, and you stop feeding those cells what they want, they stop growing.

This intervention, of no longer giving the cancer cells what they want - glucose - studies have shown, and proven, is a way to starve those icky cells of what they most desire and need to thrive, which has a deadly impact on their growth.

And in some cases, the lack of glucose can have deadly effects on a cancerous cell. And that is awesome news!

A metabolic intervention against cancer simply means that by changing the

metabolic or energy state of the body at a cellular level, one can potentially disturb a cancerous cell by starving it of those things that make it grow.
https://www.ncbi.nlm.nih.gov/pmc/articles/PMC3941741/

SUMMARY
In this section, you learned
- The Keto Diet is a low carb, high-fat diet that turns your body (or your canine's body) into a fat-burning machine.
- Keto, the diet, restricts the intake of sugar and starchy foods.
- A Ketogenic Diet is designed to induce nutritional ketosis.
- Nutritional Ketosis is a state of health in which your body is efficiently burning fat as its primary fuel source instead of glucose or sugar.
- When undergoing a Ketogenic Diet, you are essentially converting yourself from a "sugar burner" to a "fat burner."
- A metabolic intervention is a change in the environment, within the body, that those pesky cancer cells no longer like.
- Cancer cells require sugar to grow.
- Changing the metabolic or energy state of the body at a cellular level, one can potentially disturb a cancerous cell by starving it of those things that make it grow - sugar.

What Does the Keto Diet For Dogs Look Like?
A Keto Diet for the canine is typically a diet which is higher in fat, moderate in protein and very low in carbohydrates.

It does not include rendered, or high heat processed fats or proteins and does not include fruits or starches like corn, sweet potato or peas, and no grains like wheat.

Now, if you head into your kitchen and check out your bag of dry, store-bought dog food, you will notice a rather short ingredient list that starts with all the things our four-legged friends are not known to eat in their Ancestral or Species appropriate diet typically. Remember, canines are carnivores. Our dogs are, at heart, meat-eaters.

It is us, humans, and the pet industries, who have opened their diet to what they are not historically meant to eat in nature, a plant-based diet. These are called fillers in the pet food world and let's face facts; they are cheap to add to dog and cat food.

So right now I want you to go and get that bag of dog food or that wet food in a can. I want you to read the ingredients because you just might be thinking, my dog food is "wheat free" due to my dog's allergies. Or I buy my dog food at the vets, so it's the good stuff - free of those nasty fillers. Well, I beg to differ with you, but I need YOU to see just what your dog has been eating in that store bought, or often even worse, veterinarian-recommended bag or can. Do you see the first few ingredients on the list?

If you don't have your dog's food yet, please put this book down, and get it. It's vitally important that you understand that the pet food industry has duped you. Pet food is a BIG business raking in $66.75 billion in the U.S. alone for 2016.

Of that $66.75 billion - not million, but billion - pet food alone earned the industry a stunning 28.23 billion dollars.

From corn to sweet potatoes to wheat products, these fillers are doing one thing in our pets' body, the same thing that happens in the human body. These fillers are converted to glucose or sugar in the body, whether canine or human. This is simply a fact. A natural process of how the body works.

Too much sugar, we all know by now, is not a good thing for anyone and has been shown to feed cancer cells. One of the first ingredients on your dog food, I am willing to bet, is either wheat, rice, corn, sweet potato or just plain old potatoes. And don't be fooled, thinking potatoes of any kind are a good substitute for your gluten intolerant, allergy-ridden bestie.

Potatoes do one thing in the body and one thing only. They are converted into SUGAR.

And we've learned in the pages of this book that SUGAR is the food on which cancer cells grow. In fact, that entire list of "fillers" from wheat to corn, to rice, to sweet potatoes or just plain potatoes, they all have one thing in common. Inside your little or big doggy's body, they are turned into sugar.

The Keto Diet is a new option that does several important things at the same time. One way the Keto Diet works is to reduce the amount of sugar in your canine's diet while increasing the amount of fats and proteins which allows the doggy (and human) body to do something amazing.

Become a fat burning machine.

Literally, instead of burning sugar (or insulin) which has become standard now for both humans and now our pets, on the Keto Diet, our pups burn fat and STARVE those cancerous cells. Or stop them from even forming. How awesome is that!?!

The focus of the Keto Diet is to have your canine friend become a fat-burning machine, and no longer maintain an internal environment for cancer to grow.

It's time to get excited about this find, this diet, and the fact that you have this book in your hands because this information can change the course of your four-legged best friend's life and YOURS.

SUMMARY
In this section you discovered
- The Keto Diet for Dogs is typically a raw diet of fresh meat which is higher in fat, moderate in protein and very low in carbohydrates.
- It does not include rendered or high heat processed fats.
- It does not include fruits or starches like corn, sweet potato or peas, and no grains like wheat or even rice.
- Dog food is full of what's known as FILLERS - inexpensive ingredients.
- The FILLERS in dog food are quickly turned to SUGAR in a dog's body.
- Cancerous cells thrive off one thing - SUGAR!
- The Keto Diet for Dogs is all about allowing you bestie to become a FAT BURNING MACHINE.
- Burning fat is the perfect way to STARVE cancer cells.

CHAPTER 2:
Introducing The Keto Diet

Before we dive into just how to start your canine bestie on the Ketogenic Diet, let's talk results.

The angels at the KetoPet Sanctuary, located 27 miles north of Austin, Texas, have had some amazing results by focusing on nutrition for dog's who have been given, an-often-times terminal, cancer diagnosis. These veterinarians, technicians, and volunteers are caring for "lost cause" cancer dogs and even have a game-plan for after their treatments - adoption.

Did you catch that?

These dogs, given a terminal diagnosis, find their way to the KetoPet Sanctuary, a 53-acre plot of land with doggy parks, water parks, inside play and living areas, plus "human-grade cancer" treatments, which by all medical accounts, should be their final resting place.

But KPS is upping the game for these furry friends and offering them hope, top-notch medical care with awesome Keto nutrition. Plus, a healthy, happy new life with a caring family - after they cure, in some cases, those pesky cancer cells. Now, that's cool.

Here's what's even cooler and should get you excited to start your dog on the Ketogenic Diet as early as today!

The KetoPet Sanctuary is reversing Stage 1 cancer in canines.

The KetoPet Sanctuary has shown that in dogs suffering from Stage 2 cancer, even with lesions, that the disease can be paused and sometimes even reversed. Wow.

And that's not all.

The KetoPet Sanctuary can help stop the growth of cancer in Stage 3 and even Stage 4 cancer cells so that dogs with this diagnosis can live a better quality of life, longer.

See, there is hope.

And it all starts with nutrition.

You may have heard the saying; we are what we think. And it's hard to argue with that statement. What we focus on does tend to grow.

But there is something even more vital to our well-being as humans, and to our four-legged friend's health, that is more often overlooked, by even the medical community.

We are what we eat.

And so are our dogs.

So, it's time to introduce your four-legged bestie to the Ketogenic Diet and start the healing process in that little - or big - body! And here's the thing, you are already doing the hard work.

See, our canine's are sensory animals. In the wild, their senses were tuned to the hunt and survival. But now, now they no longer need to hunt as we, their loving owners provide for their every need. Our dogs no longer need to focus all their senses on survival. In the domestication of our four-legged friends, we've taken care of their basic needs, and thus they now focus all their senses on one thing and one thing only. You. Their owner.

This is why your dog is happy to see you when you walk in the door. This is why your bestie sleeps glued to your side or nudges you awake, way-too-early on a Sunday morning.

Your dog lives for you. Your dog's senses are tuned in to you.

Which is why just the tone of your voice can make that tail wag or your bestie slink off til you're in a better mood.

And right now, you are doing everything in your power to help your furriest family member!

You are reading this book.

You are educating yourself. You are aligning yourself with the Ketogenic Diet, and the changes it will require, (coming up in detail in the following pages), so your bestie can be healthier, and possibly even cured of a cancer diagnosis.

See, when you're good, your canine is good.

That's the first step.

If you're nervous or upset or freaking out, your dog will be too, because your four-legged friend feeds off your energy. So, please know you've got this.

Please understand that the knowledge you are gathering here is going to allow you to easily introduce your ball of fur or elegant, short-hair to the Ketogenic Diet with ease.

Back in the section on *What Does The Ketogenic Diet Look Like for Dogs*, we discussed the ingredients that make up this new way of feeding the canine and not the cancer.

Let's review that the three ingredient groups are again right here and then start to talk specifics so that you can get even more comfy with this knowledge. But first, take a moment to pet your bestie and stare into his or her loving eyes and share "I got this. We're going to do this together. And it's going to be easy."

Remember, you are what you think. And if you think you've got this and can do this Keto Diet for your dog (or even with your pup) then you can!

It's that simple. And in sharing that knowing with your canine, you offer more than love, companionship, and comfort.

You offer your bestie a knowing that you see to every single need he or she has. Remember, your dog is tuned into you on a level we, as humans, can't even fathom. So, when you're calm, your dog is too.

Share that love right now and give a bit of gentle love (and knowing) to your bestie, as it will fill both of your hearts, and give you the needed push (plus a smile) to keep moving forward to learn this new way of being for your four-legged friend.

The three ingredients that make up the Ketogenic Diet are
• Healthy fats are the top dog
• Moderate proteins are a given
• Non-fiber carbohydrates are kept low

Don't worry, we're going to spell out each of these three "ingredients" in great detail, but the only thing of importance now is for YOU to understand that you are in control of how to ease this transition will be for your four-legged friend.

There is no need to worry, stress or freak out. Just take it one page at a time and know we've got you covered with simple to take steps.

SUMMARY
In this section you uncovered
• The KetoPet Sanctuary is reversing Stage 1 cancer in canines.
• They are pausing and, at times, able to reverse Stage 2 cancer in dogs.
• They are providing a better quality of life for Stage 3 and 4 canine cancer patients.
• The cure starts with nutrition.
• We are what we think.
• We are what we eat.
• Canines are sensory animals.
• Your dog's senses are tuned in to you.
• You can do this!
• The Ketogenic Diet is made up of three simple things - healthy fats, moderate proteins and very little to no carbohydrates.

How To Easily Prepare For Your Dog's New Keto Diet
If you haven't started the introduction to this section of the book yet, *Introducing Your Dog to Keto the Easy Way*, you might want to scroll back a few pages, as it gives a mini-foundation for what's below.

Soon, we're going to share some recipes and give you detailed specifics on what to prepare and place in your bestie's favorite doggie bowl.

But first, we need to dive into exactly
- what to feed your dog
- why measuring what you feed your dog matters, and
- what all this ketosis means inside your little canine's body - and for the cancer cells, if they are present.

What's the Point of the Ketogenic Diet?

This is a vital question to understand, as the way this diet works, if you remember from past pages, is to introduce the body (canine or human, works the same way) to a similar-to-fasting-environment where the body becomes a fat-burning machine and no longer a sugar-burning, cancer-feeding one. And there is a way to measure shift to a fat-burning machine in both humans and our bestie.

It's called Nutritional Ketosis.

> *"The key to inducing Nutritional Ketosis is ensuring that overall caloric density is controlled and that macronutrients are distributed in such a manner that healthy fats are higher, proteins are moderate, and non-fiber carbohydrates (high glycemic load or carbs that turn to sugar) are low."*
> - Pet Parent's Handbook To a Ketogenic Diet & Canine Cancer

What is Nutritional Ketosis?

To understand the Ketogenic Diet, and nutritional ketosis, we need to go to basic nutrition school for a moment and understand a few terms. Don't worry; there are no pop quizzes at this school!

Let's start with two terms.
Macronutrients and *Metabolic Pathways*.

These terms are important to understand so you can grasp how the Keto Diet will help your bestie - and you.

Macronutrients

The three main macronutrients that make up the Keto Diet are fats, proteins, and carbohydrates. All three of these nutrients have different effects on ketosis from their digestion. Each one affects blood glucose and hormones.

Fats are 90% ketogenic and 10% anti-ketogenic, due to the small amount of glucose (SUGAR) that is released when it's digested.

So, this means FATS must be monitored since 10% of fats, once in the body, will become SUGAR. And sugar feeds cancer.

Proteins are typically ranked at 45% ketogenic and 58% anti-ketogenic since insulin levels rise from over half of the ingested protein being converted to glucose. Wow!

So, this means that proteins, up to 58% of them, once digested in the body, turn into SUGAR. And, what do we already know about SUGAR? Yep, you said it! Sugar feeds cancer cells.

So, proteins must be monitored closely to remain Ketogenic. (Don't worry; we'll be showing you just how to do this very soon.)

But first, the last of the three.

Carbohydrates are of course 100% anti-ketogenic, as they raise both blood glucose and insulin.

And carbs are the FILLERS that make up most of the store-bought foods in the $66.75 BILLION pet industry, of which pet food alone earned a whopping 28.23 billion dollars.

Carbohydrates immediately turn to SUGAR (blood glucose and insulin) in the body and just like with a diabetic, can reek havoc in the body - both human and canine. So, on the Keto Diet, your pup will be mostly CARBOHYDRATE FREE.

And you can be too if you want to accept the challenge along with your bestie. As you'll be preparing this delicious fat-burning diet for your canine, you may want to consider joining this new way of eating so you too can experience more energy, healing, and health alongside your four-legged friend!

Protein and carbohydrates will impact our bodies and keep the body from transitioning into ketosis, which is the goal.

But the most important thing to understand is how these macronutrients (proteins, fats, and carbs) are being used for energy in the body.

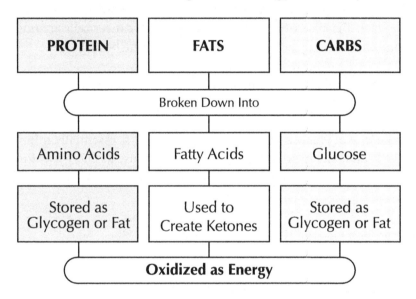

Food, in the form of proteins, fats, and carbs, are distributed in the body through our metabolic pathways after we have ingested nutrients.

Metabolic Pathways
Well, you might be asking yourself what the heck are metabolic pathways!? And that's an awesome question!

You've heard the word metabolism, which is, simply put, how the body digests, breaks down nutrients and transports those nutrients to our cells.

Metabolic Pathways are pretty much the way the body handles the breakdown
(or digestion) of fats, proteins, and carbohydrates and how the body uses those macronutrients, depending on the current "state" of our body.

There are three different states that a body can be in:
• Fed – Right after a complete meal.
• Fasting – haven't eaten in 2-8 hours.
• Starved – haven't eaten in more than 48 hours.

All three states work the same in dogs, as they do in humans, and are important to understand because this shows exactly when KETOSIS is taking place. Because when ketosis is happening, cancer cells are not being ffed, and that's exactly what we want for our canine bestie!

How do macronutrients and metabolic pathways relate back to the Ketogenic Diet?

With the lack of glucose in our systems, our body is essentially mimicking a starved state. The liver creates more ketones to use as energy, as there is less glucose (SUGAR) available – so we are using more of our FATS as energy.

And this happens for humans and our dogs. Whew!

That was a lot but remember. No pop quiz, just a basic understanding so that you and your pup can easily start down the path of a Ketogenic Diet to possibly cure that cancer diagnosis. Or stop a cancer diagnosis from every being given.

SUMMARY
Here's what we uncovered in this chapter
• The three main macronutrients that make up the Keto Diet are fats, proteins, and carbohydrates.
• Fats are 90% ketogenic
• Proteins are typically ranked at 45% ketogenic
• Carbohydrates are of course 100% anti-ketogenic
• Carbohydrates raise both blood glucose and insulin.
• On the Keto Diet, your pup will be mostly carb free.
• Protein and carbohydrates will impact our bodies and keep the body from transitioning into ketosis
• Ketosis is the goal of the Ketogenic Diet.

- Ketosis is done by putting the body into a specific state.
- The key to inducing Nutritional Ketosis is ensuring that overall caloric density is controlled and that macronutrients are distributed in such a manner that healthy fats are higher, proteins are moderate, and carbohydrates are low.
- Three different states that a body can be are
  Fed – Right after a complete meal
  Fasting – haven't eaten in 2-8 hours
  Starved – haven't eaten in more than 48 hours.
- Ketosis happens when the body is in a STARVED state.
- When ketosis is happening, cancer cells are not being fed.
- With the lack of glucose being digested (in the metabolic pathways), the body is essentially mimicking a starved state.
- The liver creates more ketones to use as energy, as there is less glucose (SUGAR) available – so we are using more of our FATS as energy.
- Metabolic Pathways are pretty much the way the body handles the breakdown (or digestion) of fats, proteins, and carbohydrates.

CHAPTER 3:
This Is What You Feed Your Dog

Bottom Line: What Do I Feed My Dog On the Keto Diet?

Great question!

If you've read the entire book thus far, you are so ready to dive into exactly what to feed your bestie. And if you're just turned to this page, that's great too, start your canine on this amazing diet, then when time allows flip back and educate yourself on the benefits, history, and science behind ancient way of eating. A way of eating that has helped countless men, women, canines and other animals heal their bodies! So, let's start with EXACTLY what you will be feeding your pup on the Ketogenic Diet.

INGREDIENTS LIST For the Keto Diet

Proteins: (raw and organic)
Ground beef, chicken, turkey, lamb, venison, duck, and pheasant.
Healthy Fats: (organic)
Coconut oil, MCT oil, olive oil, red palm oil, cream, and butter can be used as healthy fat sources.
Vegetables: (raw and organic)
Broccoli, red cabbage, spinach, Brussel sprouts, green beans and cauliflower can be used as veggie options.

The ingredients list is simple, and while there is some math involved here, once you do these basic calculations and prep for a few weeks, it will become routine. I promise. And until then, you have us, and this guide to refer to at any time!

And no, your four-legged-bestie will not get bored with the "limited" options above.

Considering your furriest family member is used to a scoop of the same dry food each morning or half a can of the same wet food, this raw food diet is going to be a delicious treat that will have tails a-waggin'.

So, I know the word math may have given you pause for a quick second, so without a moment's hesitation, let's dive into this part of the Ketogenic Diet so we remove any concern you might have about calculating your canine's meals.

Two Examples of the Ketogenic Diet

Courtesy of the KetoPet Sanctuary's booklet, *Pet Parent's Handbook For Keto and Canine Cancer,* we can provide an example of what one of two meals in the day of a couple of different dogs would look like.

EXAMPLE 1:

A nine-year-old Chow/German Shepard mix
• weighing in at 60lbs,
• with a Body Score of 6
• experiencing moderate daily activity

INGREDIENTS:
• 80/20 Raw Ground Beef   110 grams
• Coconut Oil   20 grams
• Fresh Raw Broccoli   6 grams
• Fresh Raw Red Cabbage   6 grams

Total Daily Calories (across two meals served) come in at 893kCal, with a 2:1 Ketogenic Ratio, at 15 Calories per pound.

Daily Totals
FAT: 82 grams
PROTEIN: 38 grams
NET CARBS: 1gram

EXAMPLE 2:

A four-year-old Dachshund/Chihuahua mix,
• who weighs in at 15 pounds
• with a Body Score of 5
• and experiences high daily activity.

INGREDIENTS:
• 80/20 Ground Beef   40 grams
• Coconut Oil   6 grams
• Fresh Raw Red Cabbage   3 grams

Total Daily Calories (across two meals served) comes in at 308 kCal, with a 2:1 Ketogenic Ratio, at 20 Calories per pound.

Daily Totals
FAT: 28 grams
PROTEIN: 14 grams
NET CARB: .5 grams

Now besides the ratios, grams, and calories to calculate, there are a few terms to understand first.

What in the world is a Body Condition Score!?!

But the point of sharing these recipes now is to show you just how simple it is - FOUR INGREDIENTS in the first and THREE INGREDIENTS in the last - simple. You can do this. I'm going to show you step-by-step how.

The key here is understanding how much of each ingredient to give to your dog, based on your dog's current body, health, and activity. And you don't even have to enjoy cooking to knock this Keto Diet out of the park for your canine friend!

So, let's define these terms so you can feel good about diving into some simple ratios for exactly what to feed your four-legged friend starting as early as today.

CHAPTER 4:
Keto Numbers Made Simple

The Math Behind the Ketogenic Diet - Made Easy

Sometimes math simple freaks people out and yes, there is a bit of math when putting your best friend on the Ketogenic Diet. Just like there is a bit of math when your canine is put on chemotherapy treatments, but don't worry, we're about to break it down for you.

So, let's first start with the number five. It's simple. It's easy. We can all count it on one hand.

The Five Simple Steps to Feed Your Dog the Keto Way

Step 1: Weigh your veggies
Step 2: Weigh your meat
Step 3: Measure your fat
Step 4: Mix together well
Step 5: Serve to your dog

We'll dive into exactly how you will weigh your veggies, meat, and fat in the coming sections.

But first, we hear this a lot.

Can my four-legged friend have treats on the Ketogenic Diet?

Yes, but there are no longer store-bought…they are part of what you will prepare.

Dog Treats

Consider creating a few Keto Balls by taking a two or three teaspoons of your canine's daily meal and setting it aside in the fridge as a treat during the day.

Remember, the calorie intake, and exact Ketogenic Ratio is vital to follow, so if you toss in treats that are not part of the meal plan, you may just interrupt the point of this diet - Ketosis - and the pathway to healing for your four-legged bestie.

Measuring Ingredients the Ketogenic Way

There are two terms we must understand for our canine to go Keto.

1. What the Body Conditioning Score is
2. What caloric density is and how to measure it for your pup

Let's start with the basics: Calories.

Energy is required for the body to function and is usually reported in kcal per day or kcal per gram of food.

A kcal, or kilocalorie, is 1000 calories.

This is the most common unit of energy used to express an animal's daily requirement and the caloric density of pet foods. And for humans.

Most humans eat more than 2000 kcal per day, not that we necessarily should or need to!

Standards in the pet food industry state that an average thirty-pound dog requires about 750 kcal per day. That divides out to 50 calories per pound.

And that too is a LOT!

It's no wonder much of our doggy society is overweight and overcome with cancer at increasing rates. As a society, we aren't just overeating as a whole; we are also overfeeding our best friends.

On the Ketogenic Diet, this changes, in a good way!

Our two examples above, show us that on the Ketogenic Diet, you will be paying attention to the kcal your canine consumes each day.

To do this, you need to know that on average your dog will consume 15-20 calories per pound depending on a few things - metabolism, age, health, and activity level.

Remember the first recipe for the 9-year-old Chow/German Shepard mix, who weighed in at 60lbs.

This cute girl was provided 893kCal per day.

A 60 pound older dog, with minimal activity, needs fewer calories per pound than a younger, more active dog. Makes sense, right?

So 60lbs X 15 calories per pound = a 900 calorie per day on the Keto Diet.

She was provided 893kCals which are right on target.

Remember, this is not about tossing in another fork-full of meat to get the "perfect" number, but an understanding of what works for your dog so you can adjust as needed.

Let's talk calories for the more active, younger 4-year-old Dachshund/ Chihuahua mix, who weighed in at 15 pounds.

He was given only 308kCal per day. Doesn't sound like much, right? But remember, we are talking about a small, football-tuck-able doggy here. So cute!

Now because he is 15 pounds of energy X 20 calories per pound, due to being a more active
dog, who's younger and has a higher metabolism = 300kCal per day on the Keto Diet.

Makes sense, right? So back to terms.

The caloric density is simply the energy concentration in a food expressed as kcal per gram of food. Remember, every dog's metabolism is a little different, as is their starting point on the Ketogenic Diet.

Some dogs are lean and in great shape.
Some dogs are, well, a little bit plump.
Some dogs are active.
Some are not.
Some dogs are healthy.
And some are not.

If your dog is suffering right now with cancer, the Keto Diet will look different for you, then for the dog whose owner is looking to prevent cancer.

But the good news is that it's very possible for the Keto Diet to benefit all canines, as we've shown in previous pages of this resourceful guide! To make the math easy, let's simply start at 15 calories per pound, and adjust calories up or down, based on age, weight, activity and body composition score, in response to the meal program.

Your Homework
1. You will want to obtain an accurate weight for your dog
2. You will want to ask your vet for a body condition score
3. Purchase an inexpensive notebook and keep it with you for each vet visit so that you can record the data, along with the date.

You want a running log, as well as a place to document how your pup does on each phase of the Ketogenic Diet. Plus, you may want to jot down a note or two on what you feed your four-legged friend for each meal and what is received the best! See, it might take a few tries and tweaks to get the kCal ratio perfect for your bestie, and that's okay!

Just like when a doctor prescribes medicine, often the dosage must be adjusted. Sometimes not just once or twice but several times. And that's normal.

Well, for your four-legged friend, the amount of proteins, fats, and veggies, which - math time - will be fed in a ratio, might need to be adjusted.

Why? Because remember the entire point of the Keto Diet is for your dog to experience a state of natural ketosis. This state happens when the body believes it is starved. And your canine bestie's body will be starved - of SUGAR - a good thing as far as creating an environment NOT right for cancer cells.

With this state comes ketosis, which is measured by the amount of ketones the liver produces. And remember, ketones are what the body will now use as energy, instead of glucose or sugar.

And your pup will soon become a FAT BURNING MACHINE, which is the healthiest possible state and one where cancer cells will not be happy or able to grow and often not even able to continue to live. So, your homework is to begin by getting an accurate weight and Body Score from your Veterinarian.

Body Condition Score
Let's define what a Body Condition Score (BCS) is and why it's useful.

Carol McCarty at PetMC.com states that a BCS is based on four criteria:
1. how easily felt the ribs are
2. how obvious the waist and abdominal tuck is
3. how much excess fat is beneath the skin and
4. how much muscle mass is present

Dr. Susan O'Bell, staff veterinarian at the Massachusetts Society for the Prevention of Cruelty to Animal's Angel Animal Medical Center in Boston, states that for a dog to score in the healthy range, the ribs should be easy to feel (but not see) and a defined waist, or "abdominal tuck," should be evident when your dog is viewed from the top and side respectively.

Now depending on the thickness of your dog's coat, say if you have a Yellow Lab, a vet might have to feel around a bit for a defined waist or tuck as chances are, it will not be readily visible.

Dr. Matthew Rooney, owner of Aspen Meadow Veterinary Specialists in Longmont, Colorado says, "Just as people need to maintain a good healthy body weight and condition […] a healthy BCS means that your dog is not too skinny or fat."

Rooney states that an overweight dog would have a visibly sagging stomach, no discernible waist, ribs that are difficult to feel under fat and a back that is flat and broad.

On the opposite end of the spectrum, a very underweight dog, ribs, spine and other bones would be visible from a distance.

The higher the BCS, the fatter and less healthy the dog is, Rooney says, and conversely, the lower the score, the thinner the dog is. A too-thin dog can also be unhealthy.

SUMMARY

Here's what you learned.

- Energy is required for the body to function and is usually reported in kcal per day or kcal per gram of food
- On the Ketogenic Diet, you will be paying attention to the kCal, or kilocalories, your canine consumes each day.
- The caloric density is simply the energy concentration in food, expressed as kcal per gram of food.
- The entire point of the Keto Diet is for your dog to experience a state of natural ketosis.
- Natural ketosis happens when the body believes it is starved.
- Ketosis is measured by the amount of ketones the liver produces.
- Ketones are what the body will now use as energy, instead of glucose or sugar.
- Body Condition Score (BCS) is based on four criteria how easily felt the ribs are, how obvious the waist and abdominal tuck is, how much excess fat is beneath the skin and, how much muscle mass is present.

How The Body Condition Score is Used

Scoring of the BCS is based on either a five or nine-point scale.

Using the nine-point scale, an ideal score is a four or five with lower numbers (one to three) being too thin and higher numbers (six to nine) being overweight or obese.

In general, a dog's age does not come into play when measuring body condition.

So, now that you understand what you'll be asking your veterinarian for, you can test your own amateur skills and see if your number matches what your vet says.

There is no harm in trying to measure your canine's BCS, but please understand that for best results on the Keto Diet, you will want to get a professional opinion and score.

How did these numbers work in our two previous examples?

Well, the 9-year-old has a BCS of 6 and moderate daily activity, so that implies she was a little bit overweight, not much but enough that her calorie intake was at 15 calories per pound.

While the 4-year-old little man, had a perfect score of 5 with an active lifestyle, therefore he was given up to 20 calories per pound each day.

Speaking of numbers, it's time to dive in the math or ratio of Protein: Fats: Veggies that truly make up the Ketogenic Diet. Getting the hang of this is really not that hard, it's simply new. So just follow along here and re-read as often as needed until it becomes like counting calories on Weight Watchers!

Understanding the Ketogenic Diet Ratio

The Ketogenic Ratio is not super intuitive or easy at first. But don't worry, we're going to break it down and make it as simple as possible for you and your canine!

The Ketogenic Ratio simply gives us the distribution of macronutrients for a given meal or food in this formula:

FATgrams to PROTEIN+CARBgrams

Please note that the second half of the ratio (PROTEIN+CARBgrams) doesn't tell you how much protein or carb is to be served because that is up to you.

Since we've learned in this guide that glucose (sugar/carbohydrate) is the food source of many tumor types, including cancer, carbohydrates should be very low when using a Ketogenic Diet to address cancer.

In the example recipes back in the previous section you just read, you saw a 2:1 Ketogenic Ratio for both examples. 2:1 simply means the Ratio of FATgrams divided by PROTEIN+CARBgrams

So a 2:1 Ratio means the dog received X% of calories from FAT and the rest, or X% from (Protein plus Net Carbs)

If you're feeling like your back in the classroom, you're not alone, but don't worry, you can do this!

Let's start with the math for our 9-year-old Chow/German Shepard mix, whose daily totals included 82 grams of FAT and 38 grams of Protein and 1 gram of Net Carbs with a stated Ketogenic Ratio of 2:1 in the example recipe provided on page 47.

Per the Ketogenic Ratio Formula of FATgrams to PROTEIN+CARBgrams, The math looks like this:

   82 FATgrams to 38 PROTEIN + 1 CARBgrams

or 82:39, which is as close to a perfect 2:1 as we're able to get.

See, this is NOT exact, but it is close, and more importantly, it's an UNDERSTANDING of the concept.

Your four-legged beauty or gentleman will be eating double the amount of FATgrams, to anything else, in this example. And that is what you want.

Now the Ratio of Fats to Proteins + Net Carbs can be much higher, or it can be equal.

The basic numbers are on the next page, so you can simply plug in the math to know the correct Ketogenic Ratio.

Ratio of Fat to Protein + Net Carbs	% of Calories to Fat	% of Calories from Protein & Net Carbs
0.5:1	53%	47%
1:1	69%	31%
2:1	82%	18%
3:1	87%	13%
4:1	90%	10%

A very high Ketogenic Diet would be 4:1. The average starting Ketogenic Diet, and where your focus should be, for now, is 2:1. A low Ketogenic Diet would be .05:1. The canine with cancer would start on the 2:1 Ketogenic Ratio Diet.

Now, remember, their age, current health, activity level and Body Condition Score will play a role in the Ketogenic Ratio, but for the first few weeks, you will simply test and adapt meals based on your bestie's needs.

It's interesting to note here that there have been studies published that the cancer-fighting Ketogenic Diet "formula" or Ratio - for humans - is roughly 75% fat, 23% protein, and 2% carbs. That is a 75:25 or 3:1 Ketogenic Ratio.

It is Dr. Dominic D'Agostino, an assistant professor at the University of South Florida College of Medicine, who notes that it is the underlying inflammation from these high carbohydrate diets that promote cancer, but also other diseases such as diabetes, obesity and Alzheimer's.

Your goal with the Keto Diet, whether just for your canine or also for yourself, is to focus on FATS, then PROTEINS and all but eliminate CARBS.

Why? Because carbohydrates turn into glucose during digestion and glucose is simply a fancy word for sugar. And sugar feeds cancer cells. And seems to wreak all kinds of havoc on the human, and doggy, body.

Now, it's always best to consult with a veterinarian who understands the diet, offers the best standard of care if your bestie has a cancer diagnosis, and can monitor your furriest family member through the changes - which we will dive into in the coming pages.

Along with the Ketogenic Ratio, you will be focusing on the number of calories your furriest family member will be consuming each day.

We'll dive into that next, along with some practice Ketogenic Ratio math, so you feel comfortable starting your four-legged bestie on Keto as early as today!

Summary
In this section, you dove into math - yippie! Here's what you learned:
- The Ketogenic Ratio Formula of FATgrams to PROTEIN+CARBgrams
- The cancer-fighting Ketogenic Diet "formula" or Ratio - for humans - is roughly 75% fat, 23% protein, and 2% carbs
- The Ketogenic Diet means focusing on Fats first, then Protein and just a bit on Carbs!
- Carbohydrates turn into glucose during digestion
- Glucose is SUGAR
- Sugar feeds cancer cells

The Ketogenic Ratio Cheat Sheet
The easiest way to begin to understand the Ketogenic Ratio for the food you will feed your four-legged friend is to understand that you are looking for, on average a 2:1 ratio of, for example, ground beef to coconut oil + veggies.

You will prepare all your canine meals by this Ketogenic Ratio

FATgrams to PROTEIN + CARBgrams

So, let's dive in first with a no-thought-required cheat sheet so you can do now and develop a deeper understanding as you go along.

My biggest recommendation, don't complicate this process. When your bestie likes a meal, go with it. When you feel a change in ingredients is needed, refer back to this guide and these pages and make your substitutions. Yes, some math is involved, but you will find all the heavy lifting right here in the coming chapter, that will enable you to breath easy and focus solely on your four-legged friend's health and well-being.

Ready to dive in? Good. Let's start with PROTEIN.

Ground beef is going to be your canine's staple in the coming examples, but don't worry, we'll give you alternatives and even the numbers to substitute beef for lamb and chicken.

But let's start with ground beef as this is typically a good PROTEIN source for pet-parents to start using on the Keto Diet.

See, ground beef already comes packaged with a percentage of lean meat to fat.

Maybe you know that the numbers you see on a package of ground beef - 96/4, 90/10, 80/20, and sometimes even 75/25, refer to the percentage of lean meat to fat content or maybe you don't. Either way, let's now put those helpful numbers to good use.

If you can find 70/30 ground meat, this is your best option as it's already in a 2:1 ketogenic ratio for you.

But 70% lean meat with 30% fat content, while it makes things simple, is not required and may not be easy to find in your local supermarket.

The more common option is 80/20. So, this is where we will start. With 80/20 ground beef, we will need to add extra fat to achieve the desired Ketogenic Ratio of 2:1. Currently, the ratio of 80/20 ground beef is 4:1. We can come to that by simply heading back to the classroom!

Start by removing the zeros 80/20 becomes 8/2 and then reducing that as 2 goes into 8 four times. Or 4/1 which can also be written as 4:1.

Thanks to the following chart, we can see our numbers per 1 gram of each ingredient.

Food	Amount (grams)	Fat (grams)	Protein (grams)	Carb (grams)	Fiber (grams)	Net Carbs (grams)	Cals (kCal)	Cals from Fat
80/20 Ground Beef	1.00	0.20	0.17	0.00	0.00	0.00	2.54	1.79
Coconut Oil	1.00	1.00	0.00	0.00	0.00	0.00	8.84	8.84
Raw Broccoli	1.00	0.00	0.03	0.07	0.04	0.03	0.32	0.00
Total Grams Per Day	**3.00**	**1.20**	**0.21**	**1.20**	**0.48**	**0.72**	**11.48**	10.63

If this confuses you, you're not alone. Don't worry, simply give it a quick glance then keep reading as we've created a worksheet that will break it down and give you exactly what to feed your dog.

CHAPTER 5:
Examples of Keto In Action

Four Examples of the Keto Diet - Calculated

Example 1:
Oliver is a 60-pound dog, with a body condition score of 6.
900 kCal per day at a 2:1 Ketogenic Ratio @ 15 Calories/lb.

How did we determine that we're feeding 900 kcal per day?

Our dog weighs in at 60 lbs, has a pretty good BCS (slightly overweight), and so will require 15 calories per pound. Using the Keto Meal Plan Worksheet we've created, you can plug in these numbers and do the math: (60 pounds x 15 calories per pound = 900 kcal/day)

Now, remember that all important Ketogenic Ratio we keep mentioning?

FATgrams / PROTEINgrams + CARBgrams

If we've chosen to start with a Ketogenic Ratio of 2:1, this formula should equal 2.

Using the worksheet, we've figured out that each day, Oliver should be fed:
• Ground Beef: 227.5 grams
• Coconut Oil: 33.8 grams
• Raw Finely Diced Broccoli: 24 grams

Let's explore how we got to those figures...

By filling out the example Keto Meal Plan Worksheet, we easily determined that Oliver should eat 24 grams of broccoli per day and 227.5 grams of 80/20 ground beef per day.

Because we filled in the Nutritional Information for 80/20 ground beef and broccoli, we know that each gram of broccoli has .04 net carbs and that each gram of the ground beef has .17 grams of protein. We filled those numbers in on page two of the worksheet to help determine that value of our PROTEINgrams plus CARBgrams.

Keto Meal Plan Worksheet for ___*Oliver*___ Date __*Dec 17*__

Dog's Weight	___60___ pounds

1   **5**   **9**
Too Thin   Ideal   Obese

Body Condition Score
(circle one)

1   2   3   4   5   ⑥   7   8   9

Ex: 15 calories/pound
20 calories/pound

Recommended Calories Per Pound
(based on activity level and body condition score)

___15___ calories/pound

___60___ x ___15___ =
weight   calories/pound

Total Daily Caloric Intake
(over two meals)

___900___ calories/day

Chosen Ketogenic Ratio
(based on dog's specific needs)

0.5:1   1:1   ②:1   3:1   4:1
(circle one)

Fill in the **Nutrition Informaion Chart** below based on 1 gram each of your preferred meat, oil (fat) and veggies:

Food	Amount (grams)	Fat (grams)	Protein (grams)	Carb (grams)	Fiber (grams)	Net Carbs (grams)	Cals (kCal)	Cals from Fat
Meat: *80/20 ground beef*	1.00	0.2	0.17	0.0	0.0	0.0	2.54	1.79
Oil: *coconut oil*	1.00	1.0	0.0	0.0	0.0	0.0	8.84	8.84
Veg: *broccoli*	1.00	0.0	0.03	0.07	0.03	0.04	0.32	0.0

*NOTE: Carbs - Fiber = Net Carbs

Determine How Many Vegetables to Serve Each Day:

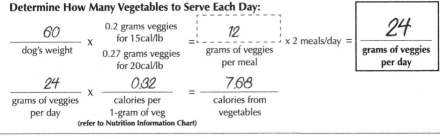

___60___   x   0.2 grams veggies for 15cal/lb / 0.27 grams veggies for 20cal/lb   = ___12___ grams of veggies per meal   x 2 meals/day = ___24___ **grams of veggies per day**
dog's weight

___24___   x   ___0.32___   =   ___7.68___
grams of veggies per day   calories per 1-gram of veg   calories from vegetables
(refer to Nutrition Information Chart)

Determine How Much Meat to Serve Each Day:

___900___   x   ___.33___   =   ___297___   -   ___7.68___   =   ___289.32___
recommended daily calories   varies depending on Keto Ratio   daily calories from meat & veg   calories from vegetables   daily calories from meat

Keto Ratio	Multiply By:
0.5:1	.50
1:1	.50
2:1	.33
3:1	.25
4:1	.20

___289.32___   ÷   ___2.54___   =   ___113.78___
daily calories from meat   calories per 1-gram meat   grams of meat per meal
(refer to Nutrition Information Chart)

x 2 meals/day = ___227.5___ **grams of meat per day**

And, once you have that number, you can use the Ketogenic Ratio Formula to determine how many FATgrams are needed.

(And you said you'd never use high school algebra again!)

We determined that Oliver needs 39.64 FATgrams in his diet. But, we know that the ground beef he's getting already includes some fat. So next, we will determine how much fat is already in the meat, and then how much coconut oil needs to be added to his food to get his ratios right.

We figure it out with just a little bit more math:

113.78 grams of meat per meal x .02 (because according to the Nutrition Information, the ground beef contains .02 grams of fat per gram of meat) = 22.76 FATgrams from Oliver's meat.

Now take the 39.64 FATgrams that he's supposed to get from his complete diet, less the 22.76 FATgrams we calculated is already in the ground beef, and you've just determined that he needs 16.88 FATgrams additional - that will come from the addition of fat, like coconut oil.

How much oil?

Take the 16.88 FATgrams you still need to add, divide it by the number of fat grams per 1 gram of oil (according to our Nutrition Information again that's 1:1 for coconut oil) and then multiply that by 2 meals a day

That wasn't so bad, was it?

Don't worry, we have 3 more examples to show you. It'll all make sense. Then, we've got a blank worksheet for you to fill out for your own dog.

And we've printed a few more blank worksheets in the back of this book because you'll need to fill out a new one for each different type of meat, veggie, or fat you decide to use in your recipes. You'll also want to repeat this worksheet if your dog's weight, BCS, activity level or anything else changes.

Determine Value of PROTEINgrams + CARBgrams (per meal):

$$\boxed{12} \times \frac{.04}{\text{net carbs per}} = \frac{.48}{\text{CARBgrams}}$$

grams of veggies per meal | net carbs per 1-gram of veggies (refer to Nutrition Information Chart)

$$\boxed{113.78} \times \frac{.17}{\text{grams protein per}} = \frac{19.34}{\text{PROTEINgrams}}$$

grams of meat per meal | grams protein per 1-gram of meat (refer to Nutrition Information Chart)

CARBgrams ____.48____
+
PROTEINgrams ___19.34___
=
PROTEINgrams +CARBgrams ___19.82___

Use The Ketogenic Ratio Formula to Determine FATgrams: (FATgrams to PROTEINgrams+CARBgrams)

Keto Ratio	Use:
0.5:1	.5
1:1	1
2:1	2
3:1	3
4:1	4

$$\frac{2}{\text{varies depending on keto ratio}} \times \frac{19.82}{\substack{\text{PROTEINgrams+} \\ \text{CARBgrams}}} = \frac{39.64}{\text{FATgrams}}$$

Determine How Much Oil (Fat) to Add Each Day:

$$\boxed{113.78} \times \frac{0.2}{\text{grams of fat per}} = \boxed{22.76}$$

grams of meat per meal | grams of fat per 1-gram of meat (refer to Nutrition Information Chart) | FATgrams from meat

$$\frac{39.64}{\text{FATgrams}} - \boxed{22.76} = \frac{16.88}{\substack{\text{FATgrams} \\ \text{still needed}}}$$

FATgrams from meat

$$\frac{16.88}{\substack{\text{FATgrams} \\ \text{still needed}}} \div \frac{1}{\substack{\text{grams of fat per} \\ \text{1-gram of oil}}} = \frac{16.88}{\substack{\text{grams of oil} \\ \text{per meal}}} \times 2 \text{ meals/day} = \boxed{33.8}$$

(refer to Nutrition Information Chart) | **grams of oil per day**

Example 2:

Sadie is a 45-pound dog, with a body condition score of 5.
900 kCal per day at a 2:1 Ketogenic Ratio @ 20 Calories/lb.

How did we determine that we're feeding 900 kcal per day?
Our dog weighs in at 45 lbs, has a good BCS, and will require 20 calories per pound. Using the Keto Meal Plan Worksheet:
(45 pounds x 20 calories per pound = 900 kcal/day)

Using the worksheet, we've figured out that each day, Sadie should be fed:
• Ground Beef: 227.7 grams
• Coconut Oil: 33.9 grams
• Raw Finely Diced Broccoli: 24.3 grams

Let's go over how we got to those figures...

By filling out the example Keto Meal Plan Worksheet, we determined that Sadie should eat 24.3 grams of broccoli per day and 227.7 grams of 80/20 ground beef per day.

Keto Meal Plan Worksheet for _____Sadie_____ Date _Dec 17_

	Dog's Weight	_45_ pounds

1 — **5** — **9**
Too Thin — Ideal — Obese
Body Condition Score (circle one)
1 2 3 ④ 5 6 7 8 9

Ex: 15 calories/pound
20 calories/pound
Recommended Calories Per Pound (based on activity level and body condition score)
_20_ calories/pound

$\dfrac{45}{\text{weight}}$ x $\dfrac{20}{\text{calories/pound}}$ =
Total Daily Caloric Intake (over two meals)
_900_ calories/day

Chosen Ketogenic Ratio (based on dog's specific needs)
0.5:1 1:1 ②:1 3:1 4:1
(circle one)

Fill in the **Nutrition Informaion Chart** below based on 1 gram each of your preferred meat, oil (fat) and veggies:

Food	Amount (grams)	Fat (grams)	Protein (grams)	Carb (grams)	Fiber (grams)	Net Carbs (grams)	Cals (kCal)	Cals from Fat
Meat: 80/20 ground beef	1.00	0.2	0.17	0.0	0.0	0.0	2.54	1.79
Oil: coconut oil	1.00	1.0	0.0	0.0	0.0	0.0	8.84	8.84
Veg: broccoli	1.00	0.0	0.03	0.07	0.03	0.04	0.32	0.0

*NOTE: Carbs - Fiber = Net Carbs

Determine How Many Vegetables to Serve Each Day:

$\dfrac{45}{\text{dog's weight}}$ x
0.2 grams veggies for 15cal/lb
0.27 grams veggies for 20cal/lb
= | _12.15_ | grams of veggies per meal
x 2 meals/day = **24.3** grams of veggies per day

$\dfrac{24.3}{\substack{\text{grams of veggies}\\ \text{per day}}}$ x $\dfrac{0.32}{\substack{\text{calories per}\\ \text{1-gram of veg}\\ \text{(refer to Nutrition Information Chart)}}}$ = $\dfrac{7.77}{\substack{\text{calories from}\\ \text{vegetables}}}$

Determine How Much Meat to Serve Each Day:

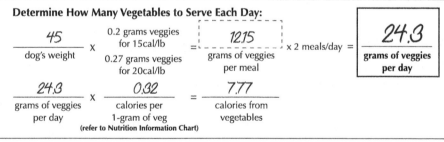

$\dfrac{900}{\substack{\text{recommended}\\ \text{daily calories}}}$ x $\dfrac{.33}{\substack{\text{varies depending}\\ \text{on Keto Ratio}}}$ = $\dfrac{297}{\substack{\text{daily calories}\\ \text{from meat & veg}}}$ - $\dfrac{7.77}{\substack{\text{calories from}\\ \text{vegetables}}}$ = $\dfrac{289.23}{\substack{\text{daily calories}\\ \text{from meat}}}$

Keto Ratio	Multiply By:
0.5:1	.50
1:1	.50
2:1	.33
3:1	.25
4:1	.20

$\dfrac{289.23}{\substack{\text{daily calories}\\ \text{from meat}}}$ ÷ $\dfrac{2.54}{\substack{\text{calories per}\\ \text{1-gram meat}\\ \text{(refer to Nutrition Information Chart)}}}$ = | _113.87_ | grams of meat per meal

x 2 meals/day = **227.7** grams of meat per day

Because we filled in the Nutritional Information for 80/20 ground beef and broccoli, we know that each gram of broccoli has .04 net carbs and that each gram of the ground beef has .17 grams of protein. We filled those numbers in on page two of the worksheet to help determine that value of our PROTEINgrams plus CARBgrams. In her case, 19.85 grams.

We determined that Sadie needs 39.7 FATgrams in her diet, and need to figure out how much of that she's getting from the ground beef so we'll know how much fat we need to add.

113.87 grams of meat per meal x .02 (because according to the Nutrition Information, the ground beef contains .02 grams of fat per gram of meat) = 22.77 FATgrams comes from Sadie's ground beef.

Now take the 39.7 FATgrams that she's supposed to get total, minus the 22.77 FATgrams we calculated is already in the ground beef, and you've just determined that she needs 16.93 FATgrams added.

How much oil is that? Take the 16.93 FATgrams you still need to add, divide it by the number of fat grams per 1 gram of oil (according to our Nutrition Information again that's 1:1 for coconut oil) and then multiply that by 2 meals a day. Done!

Want to see a few more examples? We've filled out two more for you on the following pages. Example 3 is a slightly overweight 20-pound dog named Buster and Example 4 is a very active 15-pound dog with a perfect BCS of 5 named Sammy.

After you study their worksheets, try filling out one for your own dog. It's actually a lot simpler than it looks! (And, don't worry, there are extras in the back pages of this book.)

Determine Value of PROTEINgrams + CARBgrams (per meal):

$$\boxed{12.15} \times \frac{.04}{\substack{\text{net carbs per} \\ \text{1-gram of veggies}}} = \frac{.49}{\text{CARBgrams}}$$

grams of veggies per meal

(refer to Nutrition Information Chart)

$$\boxed{113.87} \times \frac{.17}{\substack{\text{grams protein per} \\ \text{1-gram of meat}}} = \frac{19.36}{\text{PROTEINgrams}}$$

grams of meat per meal

(refer to Nutrition Information Chart)

CARBgrams _____.49_____

+

PROTEINgrams _____19.36_____

=

PROTEINgrams
+CARBgrams _____19.85_____

Use The Ketogenic Ratio Formula to Determine FATgrams: (FATgrams to PROTEINgrams+CARBgrams)

Keto Ratio	Use:
0.5:1	.5
1:1	1
2:1	2
3:1	3
4:1	4

$$\frac{2}{\substack{\text{varies depending} \\ \text{on keto ratio}}} \times \frac{19.85}{\substack{\text{PROTEINgrams+} \\ \text{CARBgrams}}} = \frac{39.7}{\text{FATgrams}}$$

Determine How Much Oil (Fat) to Add Each Day:

$$\boxed{113.87} \times \frac{0.2}{\substack{\text{grams of fat per} \\ \text{1-gram of meat}}} = \boxed{22.77}$$

grams of meat per meal

FATgrams from meat

(refer to Nutrition Information Chart)

$$\frac{39.7}{\text{FATgrams}} - \frac{\boxed{22.77}}{\substack{\text{FATgrams from} \\ \text{meat}}} = \frac{16.93}{\substack{\text{FATgrams} \\ \text{still needed}}}$$

$$\frac{16.93}{\substack{\text{FATgrams} \\ \text{still needed}}} \div \frac{1}{\substack{\text{grams of fat per} \\ \text{1-gram of oil}}} = \frac{16.93}{\substack{\text{grams of oil} \\ \text{per meal}}} \times 2 \text{ meals/day} = \boxed{33.9}$$

grams of oil per day

(refer to Nutrition Information Chart)

Keto Meal Plan Worksheet for ___*Buster*___ Date _Dec 17_

Dog's Weight	___20___ pounds

1   **5**   **9**
Too Thin   Ideal   Obese
Body Condition Score (circle one)   1   2   3   4 ⑤ 6   7   8   9

Ex: 15 calories/pound
20 calories/pound
Recommended Calories Per Pound (based on activity level and body condition score)   ___15___ calories/pound

$\dfrac{20}{\text{weight}}$ x $\dfrac{15}{\text{calories/pound}}$ = **Total Daily Caloric Intake** (over two meals)   ___300___ calories/day

Chosen Ketogenic Ratio (based on dog's specific needs)   0.5:1   1:1 ②:1 3:1   4:1 (circle one)

Fill in the **Nutrition Informaion Chart** below based on 1 gram each of your preferred meat, oil (fat) and veggies:

Food	Amount (grams)	Fat (grams)	Protein (grams)	Carb (grams)	Fiber (grams)	Net Carbs (grams)	Cals (kCal)	Cals from Fat
Meat: *80/20 ground beef*	1.00	0.2	0.17	0.0	0.0	0.0	2.54	1.79
Oil: *coconut oil*	1.00	1.0	0.0	0.0	0.0	0.0	8.84	8.84
Veg: *broccoli*	1.00	0.0	0.03	0.07	0.03	0.04	0.32	0.0

*NOTE: Carbs - Fiber = Net Carbs

Determine How Many Vegetables to Serve Each Day:

$\dfrac{20}{\text{dog's weight}}$ x $\dfrac{\text{0.2 grams veggies for 15cal/lb}}{\text{0.27 grams veggies for 20cal/lb}}$ = $\boxed{4}$ grams of veggies per meal   x 2 meals/day = $\boxed{8}$ **grams of veggies per day**

$\dfrac{8}{\text{grams of veggies per day}}$ x $\dfrac{0.32}{\text{calories per 1-gram of veg (refer to Nutrition Information Chart)}}$ = $\dfrac{2.56}{\text{calories from vegetables}}$

Determine How Much Meat to Serve Each Day:

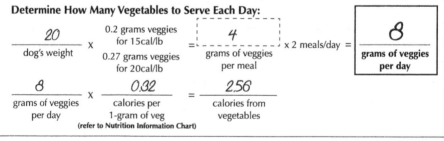

$\dfrac{300}{\text{recommended daily calories}}$ x $\dfrac{.33}{\text{varies depending on Keto Ratio}}$ = $\dfrac{99}{\text{daily calories from meat \& veg}}$ - $\dfrac{2.56}{\text{calories from vegetables}}$ = $\dfrac{96.44}{\text{daily calories from meat}}$

Keto Ratio	Multiply By:
0.5:1	.50
1:1	.50
2:1	.33
3:1	.25
4:1	.20

$\dfrac{96.44}{\substack{\text{daily calories} \\ \text{from meat}}}$ ÷ $\dfrac{2.54}{\substack{\text{calories per} \\ \text{1-gram meat} \\ \text{(refer to Nutrition Information Chart)}}}$ = $\boxed{\dfrac{37.97}{\substack{\text{grams of meat} \\ \text{per meal}}}}$

x 2 meals/day = $\boxed{75.9}$ **grams of meat per day**

Determine Value of PROTEINgrams + CARBgrams (per meal):

$$\underbrace{4}_{\substack{\text{grams of veggies} \\ \text{per meal}}} \times \underbrace{.04}_{\substack{\text{net carbs per} \\ \text{1-gram of veggies} \\ \text{(refer to Nutrition Information Chart)}}} = \underbrace{.16}_{\text{CARBgrams}}$$

$$\underbrace{37.97}_{\substack{\text{grams of meat} \\ \text{per meal}}} \times \underbrace{.17}_{\substack{\text{grams protein per} \\ \text{1-gram of meat} \\ \text{(refer to Nutrition Information Chart)}}} = \underbrace{6.45}_{\text{PROTEINgrams}}$$

CARBgrams _____.16_____

+

PROTEINgrams __6.45__

=

PROTEINgrams
+CARBgrams __6.61__

Use The Ketogenic Ratio Formula to Determine FATgrams: (FATgrams to PROTEINgrams+CARBgrams)

Keto Ratio	Use:
0.5:1	.5
1:1	1
2:1	2
3:1	3
4:1	4

$$\underbrace{2}_{\substack{\text{varies depending} \\ \text{on keto ratio}}} \times \underbrace{6.61}_{\substack{\text{PROTEINgrams+} \\ \text{CARBgrams}}} = \underbrace{13.22}_{\text{FATgrams}}$$

Determine How Much Oil (Fat) to Add Each Day:

$$\underbrace{37.97}_{\substack{\text{grams of meat} \\ \text{per meal}}} \times \underbrace{0.2}_{\substack{\text{grams of fat per} \\ \text{1-gram of meat} \\ \text{(refer to Nutrition Information Chart)}}} = \underbrace{7.59}_{\substack{\text{FATgrams from} \\ \text{meat}}}$$

$$\underbrace{13.22}_{\text{FATgrams}} - \underbrace{7.59}_{\substack{\text{FATgrams from} \\ \text{meat}}} = \underbrace{5.63}_{\substack{\text{FATgrams} \\ \text{still needed}}}$$

$$\underbrace{5.63}_{\substack{\text{FATgrams} \\ \text{still needed}}} \div \underbrace{1}_{\substack{\text{grams of fat per} \\ \text{1-gram of oil} \\ \text{(refer to Nutrition Information Chart)}}} = \underbrace{5.63}_{\substack{\text{grams of oil} \\ \text{per meal}}} \times 2 \text{ meals/day} = \boxed{\underbrace{11.3}_{\substack{\textbf{grams of oil} \\ \textbf{per day}}}}$$

Keto Meal Plan Worksheet for   *Sammy*   Date *Dec 17*

Dog's Weight	**15** pounds
1 5 9 Too Thin Ideal Obese Body Condition Score (circle one)	1 2 3 ④ 5 6 7 8 9
Ex: 15 calories/pound 20 calories/pound Recommended Calories Per Pound (based on activity level and body condition score)	**20** calories/pound
$\frac{15}{\text{weight}}$ x $\frac{20}{\text{calories/pound}}$ = Total Daily Caloric Intake (over two meals)	**300** calories/day
Chosen Ketogenic Ratio (based on dog's specific needs)	0.5:1 1:1 ②:① 3:1 4:1 (circle one)

Fill in the **Nutrition Informaion Chart** below based on 1 gram each of your preferred meat, oil (fat) and veggies:

Food	Amount (grams)	Fat (grams)	Protein (grams)	Carb (grams)	Fiber (grams)	Net Carbs (grams)	Cals (kCal)	Cals from Fat
Meat: *80/20 ground beef*	1.00	0.2	0.17	0.0	0.0	0.0	2.54	1.79
Oil: *coconut oil*	1.00	1.0	0.0	0.0	0.0	0.0	8.84	8.84
Veg: *broccoli*	1.00	0.0	0.03	0.07	0.03	0.04	0.32	0.0

*NOTE: Carbs - Fiber = Net Carbs

Determine How Many Vegetables to Serve Each Day:

$\frac{15}{\text{dog's weight}}$ x $\begin{array}{c}\text{0.2 grams veggies}\\\text{for 15cal/lb}\\\text{0.27 grams veggies}\\\text{for 20cal/lb}\end{array}$ = $\frac{4.05}{\substack{\text{grams of veggies}\\\text{per meal}}}$ x 2 meals/day = $\boxed{\frac{8.1}{\substack{\textbf{grams of veggies}\\\textbf{per day}}}}$

$\frac{8.1}{\substack{\text{grams of veggies}\\\text{per day}}}$ x $\frac{0.32}{\substack{\text{calories per}\\\text{1-gram of veg}\\\text{(refer to Nutrition Information Chart)}}}$ = $\frac{2.59}{\substack{\text{calories from}\\\text{vegetables}}}$

Determine How Much Meat to Serve Each Day:

$\frac{300}{\substack{\text{recommended}\\\text{daily calories}}}$ x $\frac{.33}{\substack{\text{varies depending}\\\text{on Keto Ratio}}}$ = $\frac{99}{\substack{\text{daily calories}\\\text{from meat \& veg}}}$ - $\frac{2.59}{\substack{\text{calories from}\\\text{vegetables}}}$ = $\frac{96.41}{\substack{\text{daily calories}\\\text{from meat}}}$

Keto Ratio	Multiply By:
0.5:1	.50
1:1	.50
2:1	.33
3:1	.25
4:1	.20

$\frac{96.41}{\substack{\text{daily calories}\\\text{from meat}}}$ ÷ $\frac{2.54}{\substack{\text{calories per}\\\text{1-gram meat}\\\text{(refer to Nutrition Information Chart)}}}$ = $\frac{37.96}{\substack{\text{grams of meat}\\\text{per meal}}}$

x 2 meals/day = $\boxed{\frac{75.9}{\substack{\textbf{grams of meat}\\\textbf{per day}}}}$

Determine Value of PROTEINgrams + CARBgrams (per meal):

$$\underbrace{4.05}_{\substack{\text{grams of veggies} \\ \text{per meal}}} \times \underbrace{.04}_{\substack{\text{net carbs per} \\ \text{1-gram of veggies} \\ \text{(refer to Nutrition Information Chart)}}} = \underbrace{.16}_{\text{CARBgrams}}$$

$$\underbrace{37.96}_{\substack{\text{grams of meat} \\ \text{per meal}}} \times \underbrace{.17}_{\substack{\text{grams protein per} \\ \text{1-gram of meat} \\ \text{(refer to Nutrition Information Chart)}}} = \underbrace{6.45}_{\text{PROTEINgrams}}$$

CARBgrams ___.16___
+
PROTEINgrams ___6.45___
=
PROTEINgrams +CARBgrams ___6.61___

Use The Ketogenic Ratio Formula to Determine FATgrams: (FATgrams to PROTEINgrams+CARBgrams)

Keto Ratio	Use:
0.5:1	.5
1:1	1
2:1	2
3:1	3
4:1	4

$$\underbrace{2}_{\substack{\text{varies depending} \\ \text{on keto ratio}}} \times \underbrace{6.61}_{\substack{\text{PROTEINgrams+} \\ \text{CARBgrams}}} = \underbrace{13.22}_{\text{FATgrams}}$$

Determine How Much Oil (Fat) to Add Each Day:

$$\underbrace{37.97}_{\substack{\text{grams of meat} \\ \text{per meal}}} \times \underbrace{0.2}_{\substack{\text{grams of fat per} \\ \text{1-gram of meat} \\ \text{(refer to Nutrition Information Chart)}}} = \boxed{\underbrace{7.59}_{\substack{\text{FATgrams from} \\ \text{meat}}}}$$

$$\underbrace{13.22}_{\text{FATgrams}} - \boxed{\underbrace{7.59}_{\substack{\text{FATgrams from} \\ \text{meat}}}} = \underbrace{5.63}_{\substack{\text{FATgrams} \\ \text{still needed}}}$$

$$\underbrace{5.63}_{\substack{\text{FATgrams} \\ \text{still needed}}} \div \underbrace{1}_{\substack{\text{grams of fat per} \\ \text{1-gram of oil} \\ \text{(refer to Nutrition Information Chart)}}} = \underbrace{5.63}_{\substack{\text{grams of oil} \\ \text{per meal}}} \times 2 \text{ meals/day} = \boxed{\underbrace{11.3}_{\substack{\textbf{grams of oil} \\ \textbf{per day}}}}$$

Now try filling out the worksheet for your own dog on the next page:

Keto Meal Plan Worksheet for _____ Date _____

	Dog's Weight	_____ pounds
1 5 9 Too Thin Ideal Obese	**Body Condition Score** (circle one)	1 2 3 4 5 6 7 8 9
Ex: 15 calories/pound 20 calories/pound	**Recommended Calories Per Pound** (based on activity level and body condition score)	_____ calories/pound
_____ X _____ weight calories/pound	**Total Daily Caloric Intake** (over two meals)	_____ calories/day
	Chosen Ketogenic Ratio (based on dog's specific needs)	0.5:1 1:1 2:1 3:1 4:1 (circle one)

Fill in the **Nutrition Informaion Chart** below based on 1 gram each of your preferred meat, oil (fat) and veggies:

Food	Amount (grams)	Fat (grams)	Protein (grams)	Carb (grams)	Fiber (grams)	Net Carbs (grams)	Cals (kCal)	Cals from Fat
Meat:	1.00							
Oil:	1.00							
Veg:	1.00							

*NOTE: Carbs - Fiber = Net Carbs

Determine How Many Vegetables to Serve Each Day:

_____ X (0.2 grams veggies for 15cal/lb / 0.27 grams veggies for 20cal/lb) = [grams of veggies per meal] x 2 meals/day = **grams of veggies per day**

dog's weight

_____ X _____ = _____
grams of veggies per day   calories per 1-gram of veg   calories from vegetables
(refer to Nutrition Information Chart)

Determine How Much Meat to Serve Each Day:

_____ X _____ = _____ - _____ = _____
recommended daily calories   varies depending on Keto Ratio   daily calories from meat & veg   calories from vegetables   daily calories from meat

Keto Ratio	Multiply By:
0.5:1	.50
1:1	.50
2:1	.33
3:1	.25
4:1	.20

_____ ÷ _____ = [grams of meat per meal]
daily calories from meat   calories per 1-gram meat
(refer to Nutrition Information Chart)

x 2 meals/day = **grams of meat per day**

Determine Value of PROTEINgrams + CARBgrams (per meal):

$$\boxed{} \times \frac{\underset{\text{net carbs per}}{}}{\text{1-gram of veggies}} = \frac{}{\text{CARBgrams}}$$

grams of veggies
per meal

(refer to Nutrition Information Chart)

$$\boxed{} \times \frac{}{\text{grams protein per}} = \frac{}{\text{PROTEINgrams}}$$

grams of meat
per meal   1-gram of meat

(refer to Nutrition Information Chart)

CARBgrams _____

+

PROTEINgrams _____

=

PROTEINgrams
+CARBgrams _____

Use The Ketogenic Ratio Formula to Determine FATgrams: (FATgrams to PROTEINgrams+CARBgrams)

Keto Ratio	Use:
0.5:1	.5
1:1	1
2:1	2
3:1	3
4:1	4

$$\frac{}{\underset{\text{on keto ratio}}{\text{varies depending}}} \times \frac{}{\underset{\text{CARBgrams}}{\text{PROTEINgrams+}}} = \frac{}{\text{FATgrams}}$$

Determine How Much Oil (Fat) to Add Each Day:

$$\boxed{} \times \frac{}{\underset{\text{1-gram of meat}}{\text{grams of fat per}}} = \boxed{}$$

grams of meat
per meal

(refer to Nutrition Information Chart)

FATgrams from
meat

$$\frac{}{\text{FATgrams}} - \boxed{} = \frac{}{\underset{\text{still needed}}{\text{FATgrams}}}$$

FATgrams from
meat

$$\frac{}{\underset{\text{still needed}}{\text{FATgrams}}} \div \frac{}{\underset{\text{1-gram of oil}}{\text{grams of fat per}}} = \frac{}{\underset{\text{per meal}}{\text{grams of oil}}} \times 2 \text{ meals/day} = \boxed{\begin{array}{c}\text{grams of oil}\\ \text{per day}\end{array}}$$

(refer to Nutrition Information Chart)

CHAPTER 6:
Monitoring Your Dog's Progress

Now each of the four examples we provided show the same ingredients, so let's talk switching out ingredients for a moment.

It's a good idea to offer alternative meat, veggies, and fat sources to your dog as a way to add variety and balance to his diet. This this is not at all inclusive of everything you can feed but it's a good list of options to start with! Just be aware of what foods are not safe for dogs (like onions, for example) and avoid foods your dog might be allergic to.

Alternative Meats/Vegetables/Fats

Raw Meat	Amount (grams)	Fat (grams)	Protein (grams)	Carb (grams)	Fiber (grams)	Net Carbs (grams)	Cals (kCal)	Cals from Fat
75/25 Ground Beef	1.00	0.25	0.16	0.00	0.00	0.00	2.93	2.25
80/20 Ground Beef	1.00	0.20	0.17	0.00	0.00	0.00	2.54	1.79
Chicken Breast, Skinless	1.00	0.01	0.23	0.00	0.00	0.00	1.09	0.11
Chicken, Ground	1.00	0.04	0.21	0.00	0.00	0.00	1.25	0.40
Lamb, Ground	1.00	0.23	0.17	0.00	0.00	0.00	0.28	0.21
Turkey, Ground	1.00	0.08	0.18	0.00	0.00	0.00	1.48	0.74
Duck Breast, Skinless	1.00	0.04	0.20	0.00	0.00	0.00	1.23	0.37

Vegetables	Amount (grams)	Fat (grams)	Protein (grams)	Carb (grams)	Fiber (grams)	Net Carbs (grams)	Cals (kCal)	Cals from Fat
Broccoli	1.00	0.00	0.03	0.07	0.03	0.04	0.32	0.00
Brussels Sprouts	1.00	0.00	0.03	0.09	0.04	0.05	0.42	0.00
Cauliflower	1.00	0.00	0.02	0.05	0.03	0.02	0.23	0.00
Green Beans	1.00	0.00	0.01	0.06	0.04	0.02	0.29	0.00
Pumpkin, canned	1.00	0.00	0.01	0.08	0.03	0.05	0.34	0.02
Red Cabbage	1.00	0.00	0.01	0.07	0.02	0.05	0.30	0.00
Spinach	1.00	0.00	0.03	0.04	0.02	0.02	0.23	0.03

Oils/Fats	Amount (grams)	Fat (grams)	Protein (grams)	Carb (grams)	Fiber (grams)	Net Carbs (grams)	Cals (kCal)	Cals from Fat
Coconut Oil	1.00	1.00	0.00	0.00	0.00	0.00	8.84	8.84
Ghee	1.00	1.00	0.00	0.00	0.00	0.00	9.00	9.00
Heavy Cream	1.00	0.37	0.02	0.03	0.00	0.03	3.40	3.20
MCT Oil	1.00	1.00	0.00	0.00	0.00	0.00	9.00	9.00
Olive Oil	1.00	1.00	0.00	0.00	0.00	0.00	8.57	8.57
Red Palm Oil	1.00	1.00	0.00	0.00	0.00	0.00	9.00	9.00
Unsalted Butter	1.00	0.81	0.01	0.00	0.00	0.00	7.17	7.17

Signs The Ketogenic Diet is Working

The Ketogenic Diet has proven to be a remarkably fast way for the body, both canine and human, to heal from all kinds of ailments, including cancer. For you and your four-legged bestie, the signs you will want to look for are going to be more medically related at first.

Of course, you want to pay attention to your doggy's stool and refer to the section in this guide, which is coming up, *Expectations of the Keto Diet*, on what to do when your canine has loose stool or vomits. These things are possible at any time, and when starting the Ketogenic Diet, please realize it's a giant shift for their little tummy.

A tummy, we might add that is created with the right gut bacteria and enzymes to break down raw meat. But like anything new, there might be some bumps along the way. Do not get discouraged; this simply means the Ketogenic Diet is working!

Now this biggest indicator that the Ketogenic Diet is working is going to be what is called Nutritional Ketosis. Nutritional Ketosis is something you need to understand as well as obtain a blood test from your vet to check - at least for the first few times.

Expectations of the Keto Diet

Your dog may experience some ups and downs, just like we do when we start a new diet. Here are a few things that could happen to your four-legged friend and what you can do to ease the way.

First, and foremost, know that with any change, there comes a bit of upset. It's okay. It's normal, in fact. So the worst thing you could do is stop the Ketogenic Diet because of a few very common side effects.

My dog has very loose stool since starting the Keto Diet. How can I fix this?

When changing from a store-bought dry food diet, your four-legged bestie may experience a short time of very loose stool. This is due to the sudden change their diet and completely normal.

If the loose stool turns into diarrhea, consider replacing your dog's meal with a slightly warmed bone broth or feed only a meal of goat's milk. A 1/2 cup of either will provide nutrients while being easy on your bestie's tummy. You can also add a small amount of pure pumpkin (in the can, not pumpkin pie filling) to their diet, as this is a natural way to firm up loose stool.

My dog is throwing up, what do I do?

Just like with the loose stool, we recommend slowly changing your best friend to the Ketogenic Diet over the course of 5 to 7 days so your doggy can acclimate to the new raw food diet.

That could look like one Keto Diet meal each day.

If you still experience loose stool or vomiting with your canine, try cutting back on the Keto meal to half of one meal split out over the course of the day for the first 3 to 4 days.

The key is to keep feeding your dog his or her normal dry food, but a lesser amount, and at a different time from the Keto Diet food.

Now some veterinarians will offer a form of over the counter acid reflux medicine for an upset stomach, but really, this should be considered a last resort.

An upset stomach, loose stool, and a little bit of vomiting is a normal reaction, and while not necessarily fun, can lead you to know you are on the right path with your four-legged bestie. Anything excessive, obviously, should be addressed by your veterinarian. But, the best way to avoid a rumbling tummy is to transition your dog to this new diet slowly.

How Will I Know When My Dog is in Nutritional Ketosis?

A few more terms to understand so that you can know if your canine is in Nutritional Ketosis.

Remember, Nutritional Ketosis is simply feeding the body the right amount of macronutrients, versus FATgrams, versus PROTEIN + CARBgrams, so your canine becomes a FAT BURNING machine, and those pesky cancer cells start to starve due to a lack of sugar.

Now, it's important to note that a FAT BURNING doggy is a CANCER BURNING canine, not necessarily a calorie-burning one who's on a skinny track!

See, often dogs with a cancer diagnosis have already lost weight. That can be one of the first signs, you the Pet Parent notices. And if this is the case for your four-legged best friend, you don't need to be nervous that turning your dog into a FAT BURNING machine will lead to a skinnier canine.

In fact, if helpful, always think of FAT BURNING as CANCER BURNING - for your pup and, for you, as proved by sciences at the start of the 20th century (and noted within earlier pages of this very book)!

So now, let's dive into these three terms.

1. Glucose
2. Ketones
3. Metabolism

Glucose (also known as sugar, are an energy source in the body) and Ketones (produced in the liver appear when FATS are broken down for energy) are measured in the blood.

Your veterinarian can take a simple blood test to share with you what your bestie's numbers are for both glucose and ketones.

But one test will not be enough for you to know if your dog is in Nutritional Ketosis.

And remember, it's only when you four-legged friend's metabolism is burning fat and not sugar that cancer cells, if present, can begin to be starved off. This is the goal!

But that doesn't mean you must take daily trips to the Vet's office and pay for a blood draw. You can actually do this at home easily.

We recommend, however, that you first start with a blood draw from your veterinarian.

Why? Simple. This will give you a true look at your canine's glucose and ketone numbers right now, without any room for doubt that you're doing something wrong. You will learn more about ketones in the coming pages.

Plus, having a few blood draws allows you to have a conversation with your vet and see if your pup's doctor is onboard with the Ketogenic Diet, or not as knowledgeable as you'd hoped, on the topic of doggy nutrition.

It happens. Some veterinarians, like some medical doctors, do not see the connection between food and health, and it's unfortunate.

But it is what it is. So, if you need to find a vet who understand's the connection between health, cancer, and nutrition, please do not be surprised.

Also, remember what we talked about earlier in this book. Often our veterinarians are receiving a lot of money by stocking their shelves with dog food that, in fact, is full of the fillers the Ketogenic Diet requires your dog to avoid. But try first, with your current veterinarian, if you have a good relationship and appreciate the care given to your four-legged friend.

You can offer this book as a way to "bridge the gap of understanding" when you bring up your canine's diet in connection with your dog's cancer diagnosis and treatment plan.

Remember, it's important to ask questions and to share a bit of information, then consider leaving what you discovered so your vet could look over the material on his or her own time, not during a 15-minute doggy focused appointment, in a jam-packed day.

Consider leaving a copy of this book with your veterinarian and stick your phone number on a Post-It note just on the front page to make it super easy for your vet to contact you after reading. Your vet might be interested in learning about this - if given the chance.

Remember, 'we don't know what we don't know,' and while your veterinarian is highly educated, nutrition of animals might not have been the focus of his or her medicine based education.

But after reading these pages, you know that nutrition is a key factor in the health of your canine, then stand firm in your belief, share the studies in this book and the successes, keep learning and work to get your veterinarian onboard for this journey.

SUMMARY
In this section you discovered
- What to do if your dog has an adverse reaction to going Keto
- Understanding that it's normal for your canine to experience some stomach upset during this transition period
- FAT BURNING equals CANCER BURNING machine
- Starving cancer cells of SUGAR is the key to stopping their growth and often terminating the defective cells completely
- Glucose (also known as sugar, are an energy source in the body)
- Ketones (produced in the liver appear when FATS are broken down for energy) are measured in the blood
- The goal is Nutritional Ketosis for your canine friend
- It's important to get your veterinarian on board with understanding the nutritional factor of your dog's care

Can I Self Test My Dog's Blood Glucose & Ketones Levels?
The simple answer is yes. More on that in a second.

First, it's important to understand that dogs are naturally primed to run on Ketones and will quickly use up what is available to them. Which is a good thing. It's like the gas in a gasoline guzzling monster truck. If it's there, it's used to power the beast, so that monster truck can move forward and well, up and over things in a powerful way.

Ketones push your canine forward toward great health, naturally. Meaning, your dog will naturally guzzle them up - and they will be helping in the cancer fight - but that may not leave enough for a true test.

Why? Because your four-legged friend may just use them up as fast as the liver can produce them. And that's GOOD. All it means is that testing your dog's ketones is not always an accurate showing of what's happening in your metabolism and body at the moment.And remember, testing blood is all about a specific snapshot in time for right now.

What You Need To Home Test Ketone Levels

Two meters you can readily purchase that are relatively inexpensive are the PortaChek or Precision Xtra Glucose/Ketone Meter.

But again, start with a blood test at your local vets to get an accurate read and consider a second ten days to two weeks after starting your four-legged friend on the Keto Diet. While it's important to keep in mind that these tests give you only a snapshot of your dog's blood levels, they can act as a handy barometer of your best friend's metabolism.

Here's what to look for in glucose and ketone measurements:

Measurement 1:
Blood Glucose 110 mg/dL, Blood Ketone 0.1 mM = NOT Ketosis

Measurement 2:
Blood Glucose 78 mg/dL, Blood Ketone 0.4 mM = Nutritional Ketosis

How often should I measure my dog's blood glucose and blood ketone levels?

Starting out, you may wish to test your dog's blood glucose and blood ketone levels often (a few times a week) as you are transitioning and optimizing their meal plan. Once you observe consistent ketone/glucose numbers, you may elect to measure less frequently, only one or twice per week.

What You Need to Test Your Dog's Blood Glucose & Ketone Levels

Glucometer/Ketone Meter
Blood Glucose and Blood Ketone strips
28G Needle or Lancet
Paper Towel

How to Test Your Dog's Blood Glucose & Ketones

Step 1: Look to see if your dog's elbows are calloused. If they are, that will be the easiest place to check their levels.
Step 2: Gently hold your dog
Step 3: Put the strip in the meter

Step 4: Take the lancet and draw a small bead from the elbow or ear and
place the ketone/glucose strip on the bead

Step 5: Wait for the beep and read the meter

If you're feeling uneasy about this process, you can find helpful example
videos on YouTube.

Is My Dog in Nutritional Ketosis?

A good indication that your four-legged friend is in ketosis would be
observed by their blood Ketones ranging from .3mMol to 1.4mMol, and
blood Glucose between 50mg/dL and 90mg/dL.

Of course, these are very rough estimates, but they can act as a handy
measure of your best friend's metabolism.

Sometimes it's easier to start by understanding when your canine is NOT
in Nutritional Ketosis. So, 0.1mMol blood Ketones and a blood Glucose of
110mg/dL means your dog is not in Nutritional Ketosis.

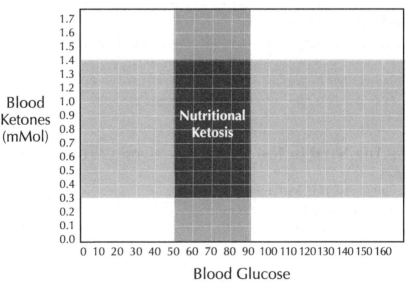

Blood Ketones (mMol)

Blood Glucose (mg/dL)

CHAPTER 7:
Success Stories Using Keto

A Doggy Success Tale

In an article published online, *Ketogenic Raw Food Diet Helps Dogs and Cats Fight Cancer And Live Longer: Keto Reverses Cancer and Boosts Longevity,* by Samantha Chang, animal researcher Thomas Sandberg says the keto diet can reverse cancer in dogs and cats and help them live significantly longer.

Sandberg, founder and CEO of Long Living Pets Research in Oakley, Utah, said his 15 years of research indicates a raw, grain-free Ketogenic Diet dramatically boosts longevity for dogs and cats. Sandberg, who launched a 30-year research project in 2000, has been tracking the health of 1,000 dogs around the world.

A lifelong animal lover who has six dogs and two cats, he started his research project because he wanted to learn how to extend the lives of his pets. "I have fed my Great Danes a Ketogenic raw food diet since 2000," he said.

"Every year my dogs undergo a full medical check-up and each year, without exception, they have been 100% healthy. There's no reason why all dogs can't enjoy a long, healthy, disease-free life with the proper nutrition." Sandberg, who himself follows a Ketogenic Diet, said his research also shows dogs placed on a Ketogenic Diet were able to completely eradicate their tumors and become cancer-free.

The cancer-inhibiting effects of a Ketogenic diet have been studied for years by leading researchers such as Dr. Thomas Seyfried of Boston College. In an interview with the Examiner, Dr. Seyfried said his decades of research indicate cancer is a metabolic — not a genetic — disease.

And the best way to treat a metabolic disorder is through diet, not by pumping a patient full of toxic radiation. Seyfried published his findings in his ground-breaking book, *Cancer as a Metabolic Disease.*

Alex's Success Story:

Alex is a 90-pound pit bull/American Staffordshire terrier mix that is ten years old (2013). He was diagnosed with osteosarcoma that had not yet metastasized. His vet informed him the options were amputation, chemo, and radiation.

Alex was in pain and had a severe limp, barely putting weight on that leg. His owner switched Alex to an all raw food diet, removed all the sugar and carbs out of the diet. Within three months the tumor was hardly noticeable. The only bump left is scar tissue in the exact spot where a biopsy was taken. May 2015, 1 1/2 years later the dog is happy and running around like nothing ever happened.

He was initially given 2-3 months to live if not having the leg amputated, chemo, and radiation. Bone cancer can be very stubborn and slow to heal, in this case, it happened rather fast.

https://longlivingpets.com/cancer-and-pets/testimonials

CHAPTER 8:
Your Keto Shopping List

Basic Items Will You Need For Your Keto Canine

- Stainless Steel Feeding Bowls
- Kitchen Scale (digital preferred with ability to measure in grams)
- Stainless Steel Spoons
- Freezer Safe Food Storage Container
- PortaChek or Precision Xtra Glucose/Ketone Meter.
- Meat (thawed and raw)
- Veggies (raw and finely dice or pureed)
- Fat Source

The Best Places To Get Your Keto Diet Supplies

Amazon often has good deals, plus free and fast shipping for Prime Members.

DogingtonPost.com is a world-renowned reference for great products and recall information.

Your Keto Shopping List

- A Digital Scale to Measure in Grams
- Measuring Spoons
- Stainless Steel Mixing Bowls
- Stainless Steel Dog Bowl
- Glass Food Storage Containers - These can be used as storage containers and are safe to put in freezer.
- Stainless Steel Spoons
- Dedicated Cutting Board For Keto - Reduce the risk of cross-contamination.
- Blood Ketone Testing Kit
- Blood Glucose Test Strips

CHAPTER 9:
Preparing Your Dog's Food

Preparing Your Canine's Ketogenic Diet - Simplified

It's very easy to get so busy and run out of time for anything in our life. Whether its meaning to go to the gym but running out of time, wanting to write a book but never finding the time to do it. The one thing we are always able to do is to find an excuse for why we don't have the time to do what we say we want to do.

Let's face a hard fact. When something is important to us - WE FIND THE TIME. When something matters to us, no matter what else is taking place in our world - WE FIND THE TIME. So, it's up to you to decide right now, to find the time to go Keto for your dog, or even with your dog - or find a reason, an excuse, not to.

The decision is yours. But you are here for a reason. We know you love your four-legged best friend or you wouldn't still be reading. We know you want the very best for your little ball of furry or your elegant, short-haired prince (or princess). We know you care.

And we care, that's why we want to share with you the very best way you can ready yourself to go Keto for your dog.

Will it take time? Yes.
Will it require some work? Yes.
Will it be hard? Only as hard as you make it.

We have spent countless hours reaching, writing, editing, and creating so that you can learn from our trial and error. We want to make this process as easy for you as humanly possible, but please understand we can not crawl out of the pages of this guide and into your kitchen to order, prep, feed and clean up for you.

That would be some magic trick, though, wouldn't it!?!

So, let's talk about what we can help you do so that you learn how to easily carve out the needed time and make your dog's Keto. You have options: do it yourself or find the meals pre-made.

Neither is right or wrong; it's simply deciding what is best for you!

OPTION 1: Prepare in Bulk, So You Aren't Overwhelmed
OPTION 2: Find a Good Commercial Source of Keto Product

Let's dive into **OPTION 1.**

Prepare in Bulk, So You Aren't Overwhelmed

Imagine that Sunday you take a day of rest. Maybe Sundays are a family day or a day to go to church or have a get-together with friends. Imagine two hours of your Sunday are spent Keto-ing.

Think you could spare two-hours? It might not even take you that long. Or, at first, it might take you a bit longer.

Remember, repetition is the mother of all skill, so expect to be a bit slow at Keto-ing the first few Sundays (or pick any day where you can carve out two to three hours) you give it a go.

I know you're asking what the heck Keto-ing is and it's a great question.

Keto-ing is preparing your dog's keto meal plan for the week. Fun, huh?!

Remember, you must have fun with this process, or you won't want to do it again next week.

Here are the Pre-Steps to Bulk Keto-ing
1. Have ingredients for the coming week of Keto Meals
2. Know the number of Keto Meals your canine needs

If you are preparing for seven days, and your four-legged friend is in tune with the Ketogenic Diet, you will need fourteen meals.

(Remember each recipe is calculated at two meals a day.)

And you have the option of giving just one meal a day to your four-legged friend, which might be a great way to ease into the Ketogenic Diet if this is your pup's first time.

This means that one meal will be Keto and one will remain store-bought, dry or wet food.

This plan also allows you to use up the dog food you've purchased and Bulk Keto enough food for 14 days, at one meal per day. Don't worry; you'll be freezing your Keto Meals.

3. Have your basic Keto supplies (found in *Basic Items Will You Need For Your Keto Canine* section)
4. Know your numbers (FATgrams to PROTEIN + CARBgrams) for one day / two meals of the Ketogenic Diet

From there you will simply multiply that number by seven if you are creating a weekly Keto Meal Plan for your canine.

Now you're ready to your two-hour Sunday (or any day) Keto-ing.

Keto-ing Once a Week Makes the Meal Planning Easy

So, if you're ready to start Keto-ing, which means getting down and dirty in the kitchen with your raw meat, choice of fat and some chopped veggies, you've already gone through your Pre-Keto-ing Steps.

You have your ingredients, your basic Keto supplies, and you know your Ketogenic Ratio numbers. (and if you don't - it's okay, we've created a handy worksheet to help you figure that all out!)

Now comes the easy, fun part. The shopping is done. The Keto Math is done. Now you get to put on some music, give your four-legged friend his favorite squeaky toy and grab those stainless steel bowls, utensils, digital kitchen scale and your raw ingredients.

Don't have a clue about the bowls, utensils and digital kitchen scale?

Check out the section entitled *Your Keto Shopping List*!

Let's take this Keto-ing Baby to the Bulk, shall we? Let's do the keto math and whip up seven days (or 14 if your pup is only eating one Keto meal a day) worth of delicious raw food.

Five Important Tips To Keto-ing In Bulk

1. You will be working with raw meats.
If the meat is frozen, make sure to thaw ahead of time. Please refrain from using the microwave to defrost the meat as this "cooks" the meat and defines the purpose of going raw!

If you need to thaw forgotten meat, the best option is to put it in a sealed ziplock bag, make sure the seal holds, and place the sealed frozen meet in a bowl of cool water - not warm, not hot.

2. Take the thawed meat out last and add it last.
Meaning, prep your veggies, first. Measure your fat, second. Then bring it home by measuring and adding the raw meat.

3. Once that meat is out, you want to work quickly.

4. You will add in the meat last, stirring the mixture and then use your digital kitchen scale to measure out precise meals.

5. Each meal should be individually stored in the freezer and thawed out ahead of time.
Today's meal(s) and tomorrow's meals can be left in the fridge, but the rest are to be placed in the freezer to prevent spoiling.

Taking a Ketogenic Recipe & Preparing it in Bulk

Let's do the numbers first. Remember the Keto Meal Plan Example on page 62 for our 20-pound canine friend?

Below are the ingredients with four protein options:

2:1 Ketogenic Ratio, 15 Cals/lb Morning Meal	70/30 Ground Beef	80/20 Ground Beef	Lamb	Chicken
Raw Meat (grams)	135.00	116.5	114.0	132.0
Coconut Oil (grams)	0.00	17.5	14.5	15.5
Raw Finely Diced Vegetables (grams)	12.0	12.0	12.0	12.0

2:1 Ketogenic Ratio, 15 Cals/lb Evening Meal	70/30 Ground Beef	80/20 Ground Beef	Lamb	Chicken
Raw Meat (grams)	135.00	116.5	114.0	132.0
Coconut Oil (grams)	0.00	17.5	14.5	15.5
Raw Finely Diced Vegetables (grams)	12.0	12.0	12.0	12.0

This is super cool. Now, please when Keto-ing, only work with one protein for the seven days you are preparing.

Why? Less risk of cross-contamination.

But also, less chance of confusing yourself with the math, ingredients and the sometimes-challenging Ketogenic Ratio!

It's a great idea to switch up protein the following Keto-ing Prep Day as this is a great way to naturally balance FATS in your dog's diet.

This chart above is two meals. So let's total the numbers for seven days or 14 meals - as this will be normal for your Keto-ing day.
First, a basic conversion that will help you immensely!

There are 453.59 grams in 1 pound.

I don't know about you, but I've never seen 70/30 ground beef, so I'm going straight for the 80/20 numbers.

Now let's calculate how much raw meat, coconut oil, and veggies we need for 14 meals or 7 days worth of Keto Meal Planning:
Raw meat (grams) 116.5 (per meal) x 14 meals = 1,631 grams

Ground 80/20 Beef:
1,631 grams / (divided by) 453.59 grams (1 pound) = 3.6 pounds

Coconut Oil:
17.5 grams per meal x 14 meals = 245 grams
Raw Finely Diced Broccoli:
12 grams per meal x 14 meals = 168 grams

Mix those three ingredients together. And then using your digital kitchen scale, you will need to quickly measure out each meal (serving size) and place it in a container that will then go in the freezer.

One meal of 80/20 Ground Beef/Coconut Oil/Broccoli is 146 grams. So, 146 grams of your delicious, raw Ketogenic Diet meal will go in a glass or chemical free plastic storage container and then in the freezer.

Now, remember, this measurement is only right for YOU if your four-legged bestie is getting 15 calories per pound and weighs in at 20 lbs with an active lifestyle and a BCS of 5.

This is simply an example based on the calculations in this chart:

2:1 Ketogenic Ratio, 15 Cals/lb Morning Meal	70/30 Ground Beef	80/20 Ground Beef	Lamb	Chicken
Raw Meat (grams)	135.00	116.5	114.0	132.0
Coconut Oil (grams)	0.00	17.5	14.5	15.5
Raw Finely Diced Vegetables (grams)	12.0	12.0	12.0	12.0

2:1 Ketogenic Ratio, 15 Cals/lb Evening Meal	70/30 Ground Beef	80/20 Ground Beef	Lamb	Chicken
Raw Meat (grams)	135.00	116.5	114.0	132.0
Coconut Oil (grams)	0.00	17.5	14.5	15.5
Raw Finely Diced Vegetables (grams)	12.0	12.0	12.0	12.0

Remember, in your Pre-Keto-ing Step; you will need to calculate how much your canine bestie must eat based on YOUR dog's weight, body condition score, and current state of health, plus activity.

Check out the section in this book on *Body Condition Score and The Ketogenic Ratio* to get a deeper understanding.

Now let's explore **OPTION 2: Find a good commercial source for your dog's keto meals.**

Preparing your own ketogenic raw dog food at home can be a bit overwhelming. We get it.

If your head's spinning, don't give up your hopes of switching your dog to a keto diet just yet. There are high quality prepared commercial options available that still comply with a ketogenic diet for dogs that make it easy for fido to go Keto!

Freeze dried raw, meat-based dog food with a vital mix of nutrient rich organ meats is one of the easiest-to-feed options on the market. Designed for pet parents who want the convenience of a traditional dog kibble with all the health benefits of a raw food. TruDog's Feed Me freeze dried raw dog food and Boost Me raw dog food booster are both excellent options for the keto diet dog.

With TruDog's freeze dried raw products, it's easy to go raw, without the thaw. There's no need to refrigerate, just reseal the bag and store it in a cool dry place. You can mix it in with other ingredients or feed it alone as an AAFCO compliant complete diet.

You can choose to add water to the food if your dog has been eating kibble, which can contain up to 70% water. Since there are no grains or any other fillers, TruDog's food will maintain it's crunchy consistency that dogs love.

Feed Me is a line of freeze dried raw dog foods and Boost Me is a raw dog food topper in shredded form that can be added to any meal as an enhancer, snack, or mix-in supplement.

Simply choose the product that suits you and your dog's needs:

Feed Me Crunchy Beef Bonanza has the proper ratio of fat to protein necessary to sustain ketogenesis with crude protein of 41.00% and crude fat of 28.00%. It contains 184 kcal per ounce.

Feed Me Crunchy Munchy Gourmet Gobbler contains turkey with crude protein of 46% and crude fat of 15%. It has 109 kcal per ounce.

Boost Me Mighty Meaty Beef Booster is also a viable option for mixing into your homemade recipes with crude protein of 41.00% and crude fat of 28.00%. It contains 184 kcal per ounce.

Custom feeding plans for your dog are also available by contacting the company directly. Simply email a TruDog Happiness Concierge at support@trudog.com or call (800) 476-8808 to get yours. Reference this book with code KETO for you best deal of up to 50% off their products. Call in orders only.

Don't miss $100 worth of valuable coupons so you can try TruDog with your dog - they're found in the back of this book!

CHAPTER 10:
Feeding a Raw Diet

Working With Raw Meats

There may be bacteria in raw meats, and you will need to be diligent in prepping your food, cleaning and food storage (for preparing your canine's Keto meals in bulk).

Let's first talk about the risk for your dog when eating raw meat.

Yes, there are pathogens and bacteria in raw meat. Your canine has saliva containing lysozyme, an enzyme that destroys this bacteria.

It's worth pausing for a moment to share that there are going to be so many benefits to Keto for your canine bestie besides fighting cancer and other ailments. And you should be excited by this knowledge.

For example, once off store-bought, carbohydrate-high dry or wet dog food, the amount of plaque on your four-legged friend's teeth will diminish. You may also notice your dog has more energy, a shinier coat, healthier skin, and smaller, less-stinky poop!

So, yes, there is prep, and there is the need to keep your kitchen clean after preparing your dogs Ketogenic Diet, but the benefits you will see in your furry friend will make it all worthwhile.

7 Steps to Cleaning After Prepping & Serving Raw Meat

Okay, I think it's safe to say that we all clean up our kitchen after preparing a tasty meal - whether cooked or raw. But not all of us are used to prepping raw meat. That said, a few things are important so that you eliminate cross-contamination.

1. Use Stainless Steel whenever possible (dog bowls, mixing bowls, utensils)
2. Use a dedicated raw-meat cutting board
3. Consider using stainless steel mixing bowls or glass containers to freeze and store your prepared Keto meals
4. Sanitize your kitchen counters; your raw meat dedicated cutting board, utensils, mixing bowls and dog bowls
5. Wash your dog's bowl immediately after each meal
6. Leave your dog's food dish down only long enough to eat. If your dog is not hungry or interested, it's okay. Simply cover the dish and put it in the

fridge and try again later. (See *Tips For When You Canine Does Want To Eat*)

7. Consider taking one day each week to prep all your dog's Ketogenic Diet meals for the coming week.

This will make prep, clean up, and feeding a breeze.

Simply freeze the meals in individual containers, separated by meal (if feeding AM/PM). Each night put two meals in the fridge so the food will start to thaw out for the next day.

Do I Need to Worry About Bacteria Too?

This is a valid concern for a lot of new Keto-feeding doggy parents.

You should handle your dog's raw food in the same way you would handle your own raw chicken or hamburger patties - by storing it in sealed containers and freezing it until you're ready to use it. This will help deter bacterial growth and reduce spoiling.

If you keep your prep area clean, your doggy bowls and the area around them sanitized after each meal, and wash your hands after you handle the food, you should be just fine.

Here are four easy steps to follow to help you feel comfortable handling raw meat with your four-legged canine:

4 Simple Steps To Minimize Bacteria Risk

1. Leave food down only as long as it takes your dog to eat
2. Immediately clean and sanitize the food bowl
3. If food is not eaten right away, put it in the fridge for later
4. Keep the area around the food bowl sanitized (see *Bonus Recipes* for an all-natural cleaner)

Can I Just Cook the Raw Meat?

Cooking protein does two things. It adulterates the fat contained in the meat, and it can increase caloric density by making the meat more bioavailable.

Dogs are very well equipped with the right type and amount of gut bacteria and enzymes to naturally break down raw food. Also, dogs are not able to digest cooked animal fats as we do and this can actually increase the risk of pancreatitis for our four-legged friends.

Keeping it raw is actually the form in which your bestie would consume fats and proteins in the wild.

What About the Organs...And Bones?

When you first start out on the Ketogenic Diet with your bestie, don't worry about the organs and bones. Here's why.

Too much information can be overwhelming and can freeze you in your tracks.

Start simple with the recipe shown in the previous pages - raw meat, healthy fats (typically oils) and some veggies.

If you do an online search, you will find tons of information about feeding your dogs a RAW diet, and while that's good, it's a bit like the cereal aisle in the grocery store. Too many options can be SO overwhelming.

So the key thing to remember here is yes, you are going RAW with your four-legged friend. But more importantly, you are going KETO RAW.

The point right now is about making your dog a FAT BURNING or CANCER BURNING machine if your dog has been diagnosed. And if there is no cancer, setting up a healthy lifestyle that will allow your bestie to live a long, happy life - disease free.

Yes, the organs and bones are an important part of a raw diet for a dog. Yes, you should consider adding them in for nutritional balance, however, start slowly the first few days or even the first few weeks - if the idea of organs or bones concern you.

Organs are some of the healthiest, most nutrient-rich foods that your dog can consume. Raw, uncooked bones provide a good cleaning of the teeth, exercise of the jaw, the needed calcium for good health; and so much more. So when you're ready, there are a few things you can easily do to add organs and bones to your dog's diet.

Consider adding organs, like kidney, liver, spleen, or pancreas to your protein mixture. If you need 130 grams of raw beef, consider allowing 10% of that mixture to be replaced by organ meat. (But never use more than 5% liver because it's so high in Vitamin A and will cause diarrhea if your dog consumes too much of it.)

Remember, this is key. You can't add more protein to your 130 need grams for the meal; you must keep your ratios to stay on the path to allow the doggy body to produce Ketones.

That said, if you needed 130 grams of raw ground beef and wanted to add 10% organs, you would remove 13 grams of ground beef and replace it with 13 grams of ground or chopped organs.

A bonus is that dogs usually love the taste of organs, and, while you may get some unusual looks from the butcher when you ask for them, they are very inexpensive cuts of meat to buy!

Just a side note, this might come as a surprise, but heart is actually not considered an organ when we're talking about a raw diet, think of it as another muscle.

If you want to include raw bone in your bestie's diet, first consider offering raw meat bones as treats a few times per week. You can ask your local butcher or supermarket for duck necks, turkey necks, and lamb necks.

Lamb necks can be given as a treat but should be taken away when they reach 1-2" in diameter, so your dog doesn't risk swallowing them.

Duck and turkey necks can be eaten as a whole meal as a dog can fully consume them - bones, muscle, tissue and all.

Consider offering this for one meal, once a week - weigh that turkey neck and deduct the grams from your protein. Please note this calculation will not be exact as this is not just protein. at is why once per week is a good place to start.

It's also important to never feed your dog cooked bones. These become brittle and can splinter off,, causing serious injury when swallowed by a dog.

Another way to provide needed bones to satisfy your four-legged friend's desire to chew is to offer a fun bone.

Not to be confused with a "funny bone!"

A fun bone is a chew toy that is healthy and natural. Great options are beef kneecaps and beef knuckle bones from a reliable source.

CHAPTER 11:
Changes in Your Dog on Keto

Ketogenic is About Quality Versus Quantity

Remember, the focus of the Ketogenic Diet is on calorie-dense food not on the amount. In North America especially, we are used to huge portions and that, in and of itself, is not healthy. For our canines, the impact of overfeeding is stress on their little joints, hips and organs, plus obesity, diabetes, and cancer.

Why Does It Seem Like Less Food?

I want to warn you before you start mixing up your first batch of Keto dog food. It may not seem like a lot of food at first.

And it's true, it is "less" quantity but stick to the measurements provided because it's not the amount of food that matters, but the nutritional density of it.

That said, remember:
1 gram of fat has more calories (9) than 1 gram of protein (4).

And the focus of the Ketogenic Ratio is FATgrams first!

Always keep your Ketogenic Ratio in mind:

FATgrams to PROTEIN + CARBgrams

What if My Dog Is Hungry on the Ketogenic Diet?

Now, if you feel that your dog is STARVING or see that after a week or so your canine is starting to shed pounds on this new Keto Diet, take a step back and make sure your dog isn't simply getting "healthier" on this new eating plan.

Remember, a typical serving of processed dog foot can in many instances range from 26 to 32 calories per pound.

On the Ketogenic Diet, we base our starting point on 15 calories per pound, adjusting calories up or down based on your bestie's weight and Body Composition Score. Unless your canine is already extremely lean, start with 15 calories per pound and simply pay attention.

Know too, that we tend to overfeed our four-legged friends, which is NOT in their best interest. That said, it might take time for you to adjust to the fact that your dog is simply healthier on this diet and, in fact, not actually starving.

Remember, before dogs were domesticated, they ate a prey-based diet and not two square meals a day, at a specific time. In fact, the .5:1 Ketogenic Ratio is more in alignment with the metabolic cycle our furriest family member might experience in the wild.

Granted, I know what you're thinking. Your little ball of fur or big boy isn't in the wild, and that's true.

Your four-legged friend is no longer exerting energy to hunt for food, take down prey or go days without eating. And some breeds never have lived like this. But a dog's natural, genetic makeup is still present.

Dogs are carnivores. They are meant to eat small, raw meals, high in fat and protein, spaced apart, with very little carbohydrates. They are meant to work for their food through hunting, thus exerting physical activity before eating. In the wild, not eating regularly, allowed the canine to enter into and out of ketosis naturally.

Chances are, your bestie will do great on the Ketogenic Diet simply because it does mimic a natural, innate cycle of going in and out of ketosis for your furriest family member.

Steps to Take
1. Weigh your dog - at the vet is best.
2. Obtain your canine's Body Condition Score (BCS)
   from your veterinarian.
3. Calculate 15 calories for every pound your dog weighs.
4. Take into consideration the BCS Score and move the calorie intake
   up to 20 for a healthy, active, good BCS scoring canine.

Tips For When Your Canine Doesn't Want To Eat
It is not unusual for a canine to skip a meal. Actually, it can be healthy for them. Remember, in the wild; they don't automatically eat at 7 AM & 6

PM. They eat when they hunt. They eat when they're hungry. They eat to survive.

Here are a few things you can actively do if you're doggy is not as excited to eat the new Keto Way.

- Exercising your dog just before feeding can incentivize them to consume their meal.
- However, should they miss three meals in a row, you may wish to switch up the protein, the fat, the veggies, and offer them a new taste profile.
- Additionally, you can try drizzling chicken broth, bone broth, or sardine juice over the food to help entice them to eat.

Give your four-legged friend time. This is new and might take a few days or a week to sink in that the dry, store-bought kibble is gone… and the treats, yep, gone too.

Consider easing in with one Keto meal per day for the first 5 to 7 days.

CHAPTER 12:
Protecting Your Dog
From Cancer

How To Protect My Four-Legged Friend From Cancer

I think it's important to first say that living in fear of cancer is not the best choice.

One, it causes stress in your body. And stress causes dis-ease. You need to be the healthiest version of yourself so that you can take care of your four-legged bestie.

Two, any stress you feel, your canine feels, too. And like we've already stated but it's totally worth repeating, stress can lead to dis-ease in the body.

Yours and your canines.

In the coming pages, we're going to dive into topics that you can explore, many of which if action is taken, could help protect your furriest family member, and possibly even yourself, from cancer.

Dive into these pages and commit to making just one change. One step, one change, can have a huge impact.

If that step is to introduce your dog to a raw food diet, well, that is a big step. In fact, going raw is a marathon, not a sprint and it doesn't happen overnight. So focus your energy there. Glance at the following pages and come back to them once your bestie has settled into the Ketogenic Diet.

Because the benefits of that diet have proven to be swift for many four-legged friends and you can read up on some of them in our Success Stories section located toward the end of this book.

General Risks For Developing Cancer - For Dogs

Nutrition

This book is all about the importance of nutrition for our four-legged friends. If you haven't read from page one, take some time and read up on just why nutrition is key for your dog's health.

Sugar

Store bought wet and dry foods are full of sugar. No, you won't see it listed as an ingredient on the bag or can. Instead, you will see it as wheat, rice, corn, sweet potatoes or potatoes. See all of these items, when digested in the doggy and human body, become SUGAR.

In this book, from page one, we go into great depth about sugar and how SUGAR FEEDS CANCER.

Glance back at the first section again or take time now to read it so you can fully understand the importance of removing sugar from your bestie's diet, so that cancer cells can be starved off.

Obesity
You may not think your pup is on the plump side, but chances are, he or she weighs in at a few extra pounds.

See it's healthy for our dog's ribs to show - just a little. Think of it as a doggy six-pack. But how often do you see a dog's ribs, except when on a commercial showing an abused animal.

There is a definite line between obese, plump, healthy and a starved animal. Much like a model on the cover of Cosmo, I'd encourage you to start to look at your dog's figure with an open eye. An eye for healthy, not the standard of normal.

Just like a rail-thin, waif of a woman, with clothing hanging off her too-thin body, is NOT the definition of healthy. We do believe, in this country, that it is a definition of beauty and therefore, normal. Something even to strive for.

There is a problem with perception. So what is the perception you have of your dog's little or big body? The key here is to start to see what's healthy for your dog, not what you see as best.

The eyes can be deceiving, along with what we believe to be healthy.

Immune System
A lowered immune system, in a human or a dog, is the breeding group for health issues.

The Ketogenic Diet is the best defense against a weakened immunity and can quickly bring your four-legged friend back to a stable, healthy place.

Genetics
Like with humans, there is a genetic favor of what our four-legged bestie was handed down from his or her dog mommy and daddy. These aren't things we can control but simply understand they are present and may play a role in the health of our canine friends.

Breeds
We know that some breeds are simply not as strong, genetically, as others. Some breeds are more susceptible to hip dysplasia, breathing issues or even the development of tumors or cancer.

It's important to know a bit about the breed of dog you have and any future breeds you plan to add to your family line - before bringing them home.

Remember knowledge is power.

Lifestyle
Is your dog active? This is one aspect of our furriest family member's lifestyle. We know active is a relative word for our canine friends, based in part on the breed and also, their current state of health.

An English Bulldog is going to be much less active than a Jack Russel or even a Cocker Spaniel. Just like a Springer Spaniel will need to run, almost as much as a Grey Hound. We know too that a Maltese only has so much energy to exert and then is down for the count - a lengthy nap.
But lifestyle factors include more than just how active your bestie is.

Lifestyle includes environmental factors from the cleaners you use on your floors, where your doggy paws are a-walking, to the water your provide, to the amount of time outdoors to the one-on-one love time.

Lifestyle is the amount of stress you feel, that in turn your dog senses, absorbs, and feels, too.

Environmental Factors

Whether the chemical cleaners used at home or the fertilizer or pesticides in the yard, it's important to remember that your four-legged friend is absorbing everything through the delicate skin of the paws.

From skin allergies to poor digestion to lumps, tumors, lesions and yes, even cancer, environmental factors play a role.

The key here is again not to stress, but to start looking first at what you use in your home environment, that could be of possible harm. It's possible to make simple adjustments there that can do a world of good for the health of your bestie (and yourself).

Curious how to clean without harsh chemicals? Or what to use in place of synthetic sprays to make things, like your pup's bed, smell fresh? Check out the recipes section for a few easy-to-make home cleaners.

Vaccinations
Know that you can ask questions when it comes to vaccinating your canine and not all dogs need to same vaccines.

Now, there is the possibility that vaccines can cause tumors and there are even those who claim they cause cancer.

This book is not going to dive into this loaded topic but simply state that it's important you know what your dog is being given, when they are being given (as some vaccines should not be mixed or given on the same day) and if you are ever unsure, stop the process and learn more.

When a Female is Spayed
It is shown that the fewer menstrual cycles a female dog experiences before being spayed, the lower her chances are of developing mammary cancer.

Why? It is thought that with each hormonal cycle or "heat" that female dog experiences, there is a mutation in the hormone that floods her body.

It's important to speak to your vet about the real possibility of mammary cancer if you choose not to have your younger, female dog spayed.

CHAPTER 13:
Your Dog Has Cancer: Do This!

My Dog Has Cancer - What Do I Do Now?

It's natural to feel disbelief, fear and even dread when you hear that you four-legged friend has cancer.

Disbelief in that it couldn't possibly be happening. Fear that your furriest family member might not make it. Dread over what's to come from understanding the cancer diagnosis to learning about treatment options and even to the cost associated with helping your bestie. All of these emotions are normal, and they are part of the cycle we feel when we receive devastating news, whether it be a family member, friend or our canine buddy.

But now you can experience another emotion - *hope*.

Hope that this diagnosis doesn't have to be the end of the road for your four-legged friend, even if your veterinarian tells you the diagnosis is terminal or that even surgery is not an option.

See, doctors and vets and trained that up believing that most diseases can not be cured. See, cancer can be stopped. Cancer can, in some cases, be reversed. Cancer, in some instances, even be cured. Do not let anyone tell you differently.

What To Do When You Get A C-Diagnosis From Your Vet?

The first thing to do when you receive news that your bestie has cancer is to arm yourself with knowledge.

We've talked about this before, earlier in this guide. Knowledge is power.

Let's be honest, a cancer diagnosis is bad. It means your doggy's health is in jeopardy. But it's also a wakeup call. And it doesn't have to be a death sentence.

It's true; we aren't vets. We didn't go to school and get the Doctorate of Veterinary Medicine degree.

We are just people. People with a passion. A deep, unconditional love for our four-legged canines that knows no bounds.

It is because of this love that we spend countless hours reading, researching and combing through articles, blogs, journals and magazines to find the information you need to make an informed decision about your next steps.

And you are doing it already. You have this book in your hand, and you are reading these words. You know, in your heart, that a cancer diagnosis for your canine does not need to be life-threatening.
You want answers, and you want help.

Well, you've got it right here.

7 Steps To Take Now That You Have A Cancer Diagnosis for Your Canine

1. Talk to your veterinarian about your dog's options (surgery, chemotherapy, immunotherapy, and radiation are often options).

2. Ask your veterinarian about any recommended nutritional changes for your pet in general.

3. Ask your veterinarian about the Ketogenic Diet. Do not be disappointed or shocked if your veterinarian does not see the connection between cancer and nutrition.

4. Ask yourself - Do I agree that there isn't a connection between nutrition, health and the cancer diagnosis of your canine bestie?

5. Consider finding a veterinarian who understands the importance of nutrition and is willing to listen even if he/she doesn't yet know about the Ketogenic Diet for Dogs that has been shown to help stop and, at times, even cure cancer.

6. Read this guide and learn all you can in these pages about the Ketogenic Diet. Start first with *Success Stories* after you finish up this section. Hope is a powerful motivator.

7. Commit to putting your four-legged friend on the Ketogenic Diet for 30 Days and monitor the results through testing of the glucose and ketones,

as discussed in detail within this guide.

Is Your Dog Healthy Enough to Go Keto?

Maybe the better question is this - is your dog healthy enough not to go Keto?

And the answer is simple. When it comes to our dogs, there is no such thing as too healthy.

Whether you have a new pup, cancer-free, and are simply reading these pages to gather information, or you have a life-threatening diagnosis hanging over your four-legged bestie's head, Keto is the answer.

Take Dejojo, a 15-year-old dog with tumor in his mouth. The vet told the owner nothing could be done. His owner refused to give up on him.

The tumor had grown too large and removing it meant removing a large part of his mouth making it impossible for the dog to chew food.

Treatment [of a raw food diet] started on November 11, 2009. Within a week the tumor had already gone down about 25%. One month later the tumor was gone!

In Jan 2011, Dejojo was 16 years old and still going strong!

Now, I don't know about you, all I know is that the love a doggy owner has for their bestie, knows no bounds.

Your canine feeds off your energy. Your four-legged friend senses how you feel and acts accordingly. So yes, take a moment to grieve the news of a cancer diagnosis. Take time to hug your doggy tight and pet that fur coat.

Then dive back into getting the best information you can to increase your canine's chances for a healthy, long life - very possibly cancer free.

If Dejojo at 15 can do it, surely your doggy has a fighting chance!

Consider the Keto Diet Over Other, More Costly Forms of

Cancer Treatment for Your Canine Best Friend

Let's face facts for a moment and simply state the truth. Cancer treatments are costly.

Even with a top-of-the-line pet insurance, your out-of-pocket expenses for surgery or chemotherapy or immunotherapy or radiation, not to mention the CT Imaging, standard and advanced blood panels, as well as tissue pathology, and vet appointment bills will add up fast.

And you might be thinking, well isn't feeding my dog raw people food expensive, too?

Sure, it is. It's more expensive than the store-bought dry or wet food that is probably in your doggy cupboard now. But if you check out the ingredients list you'll notice, even if it's vet recommended, it's full of harmful fillers.

Fillers like wheat, corn, sweet potato and regular potato that do one thing and one thing only in your doggy's, possibly sick body.

Those fillers turn to sugar. Another word for sugar in its digested state is glucose. If you know a diabetic, you're familiar with the word.

Well, here's what you might not yet be aware of it you haven't read the beginning of this guide. Sugar is what cancer feeds on.

Cancer cells don't even need oxygen to grow. Weird, right? I mean everything needs oxygen, or so we've been taught since biology class.

Well, it turns out cancer cells are different, they thrive on glucose - sugar - and can grow rapidly the more they are fed. But, here's the sweet spot. Remove cancer's food source - sugar, which is what the Ketogenic Diet does - and the cancer cells start to wither way, often as quickly as they grew.

Sounds too good to be true? It's not.

Check out the *Success Stories* in this book.

Flip back a few pages and read about Dejojo, a 15-year-old with a "nothing-we-can-do" diagnosis from the vet. See what happened to Dejojo just weeks after going raw! Yes, weeks!

Then ask your vet about what is recommended for your bestie who's been given a cancer diagnosis. What treatment plan, if any, is being offered and what are the costs involved?

We can share right now that even with regular bi-weekly veterinarian checkups and blood glucose and ketone testing by your vets, along with the Ketogenic Shopping List, you won't even come close to the costs of chemo and other medical options.

Now, don't get me wrong.Veterinary medicine has its place. Surgery is sometimes the right move. But ask yourself what you can afford, financially and emotionally, before you go with chemotherapy, immunotherapy and radiation treatment.

Watching your doggy suffer is a painful price to pay that you may just be able to avoid by reading up on the options presented in the Ketogenic Diet and this guide.

We don't claim to have all the answers. But we do know that the Ketogenic Way will not break the bank. It will require some work on your part. It will require you learn about feeding your dog a raw diet. Heck, it will even require you to do some math.

But nothing like the math and sinking feeling in your gut as you add up the medical bills of proposed treatments that come with no guarantee.

The Potential for Reversing Cancer With Any Form of Treatment - The Ketogenic Diet or Otherwise

Cancer is a scary word. It's also a common word. But should it be?

First, should we really be so afraid of cancer for ourselves and our canines? Well, let's keep this discussion focused on our canine friends, and yes we should be afraid.

Why? The numbers are rising, not decreasing. Most veterinarians are not ready to see (or willing to see) the connection between nutrition and cancer.

But we should also be hopeful. Because there is knowledge out there that you now have in your hand, even in your veterinarian doesn't have. In fact, you might want to consider gifting them a copy of this book along with a letter in 30 days when you share just how amazing your four-legged friend is doing on the Ketogenic Diet!

But let's talk about the potential for reversing cancer because that's why you're reading. You're interested in the topic because either you have a cancer diagnosis for your bestie, or you're concerned one could be in your dog's future. So, let's dive in.

Simply put the results someone (doggy or human) gets depends on the treatment used and the specific person or canine. Point blank, each specific case will harbor different results.

Every doggy's system (and every individual's system) is different from the next, and the impact that a treatment will have on a specific type of cancer can be altered due to countless other factors.

This could include the sensitivity of their condition, how progressed the cancer is, and any number of other unforeseeable environmental influences. Sometimes the body's reaction to a type of treatment may be in the form of rejection, the polar opposite of what is hoped for, which only worsens the overall condition.

Cancer can be a stubborn illness, much to the deep dismay of those affected by it. It can be incredibly difficult to find treatment with the efficiency to halt the symptoms of cancer, let alone actively fight against it. Cancer can take a tremendous toll both on the sufferers and their loved ones.

With the case of animals, there is a deep dependence on the owner that can develop into a burden as the pet's condition changes or worsens. And this can result in feelings of guilt and financial hardships, to name a few.

It is not uncommon for cancer to develop into a chronic, long-term condition. In fact, many people with cancer experience several reoccurrences and many even continue to fight the illness again throughout their entire lifetime. Some would even consider cancer to be an "intelligent" illness.

This is due to its ability to adapt and evolve within the body's systems, even while under attack from various forms of radiation or treatments.

Cancers can often disappear within the body before emerging into a different location. Cancer can reoccur or relocate even after extensive forms of treatment, as long as a few live cancer cells remain active in the body.

This can occur in a number of ways in the case of any treatment. With surgery, some cells may be left behind or have broken off into a separate cluster. With chemotherapy, cells are killed as they divide, the cells that are not in the splitting process remain unaffected. Radiotherapy attacks the cells to inhibit them from dividing.

Through any method, cancer cells can often survive. This is true for humans, animals, and pets of any kind.

Now, all this is said not to freak you out but to share the harsh reality that perhaps your vet won't when discussing surgery, chemotherapy, immunotherapy, and radiation.

See, there are no guarantees that any of those options will work.

In addition to the large toll that many treatments have, cancer can very easily resurface in a short time frame. It is almost impossible to be completely certain that every cancerous cell has been removed from the body via treatment. Even if a cancer has been eliminated, some risks for developing it again remain.

In this case, the body has, likely, already been weakened through undergoing certain dangerous treatments and is, therefore, at an even greater risk.

Yet, a case like this could be considered successful. For most cancer patients, the idea of even getting to a stage where it is a reoccurrence is but a distant possibility.

Often, through severe treatment methods, cancer is attacked to keep a tumor from continuing to grow. The hope is to halt cancer's growth and progression for a short time rather than working towards actively fighting against it in the hope of its eradication. In such a case, cancer can be controlled and stabilized for months at a time.

The condition is not quite as intensive unless the cancer begins to grow again. As the cancer develops, more treatment it has undergone to halt the effects.

Am I the only one who sees this as slightly crazy?!

The goal of most treatments is not to kill off the cancer. Why? Because the medical community doesn't really believe it's possible. Instead, it's about punching it in the face, hoping for the best and waiting to see if it comes back again.

Remission is a stage most people only hope that their treatment level reaches. Remission is described as the state when treatment has been, at least, partially effective in destroying the tumor. Usually, the cancer is eliminated, at least by half. This doesn't mean that the person, or canine, is in the clear.

Of course, each case is different, but remission can range from a reduced tumor to no tumor at all. As previously mentioned, cancer can make reappearance at any stage, and it is nearly impossible for a form of treatment to be entirely effective.

Says the medical community.

Despite the research that has been done to confirm the possibility of a cure for cancer, the Ketogenic Diet is an example of one form of treatment that has yet to be properly acknowledged or recognized, in any way, as an effective form of cancer treatment by the medical or veterinarian communities.

Let me say that again.

There is proof that the Ketogenic Diet shrinks cancerous tumors and eliminates cancer cells, and yet it's not widely known or used as a treatment method.

Doesn't that seem crazy when there is a considerable amount of research available that explores the impact of a Ketogenic Diet as a potential cure?

In 1926, less than one hundred years ago, a scientist by the name of Otto Warbug first presented dietary habits as a potential cancer cure. Remember, we discussed his work in an earlier section of this guide.

He explained the scientific process behind a tumor or cancer cell growth and found the nutritional connection. The Warbug Hypothesis explains that, like any living element, cancer cells need to collect energy from somewhere in order to survive, spread and continue to pose a threat to the body.

He showed that sugars in the body, in the form of glucose, convert into food for cancer cells to feed and thrive on.

With the Ketogenic Diet cancer cells are starved.

Warbug's hypothesis, at its core, can stand to serve as the foundation for any proof of the Ketogenic Diet has the potential as a breakthrough in cancer treatment.

Warbug even received a Nobel Prize for a similar theory he developed surrounding the habits of cells, which just goes to stand that he was certainly qualified to make such as bold statement through his hypothesis.

In spite, of any qualification or support for his research Warbug's theory still failed to properly catch on. While Keto had been used at different times for other treatments, including illness and epilepsy, it was never confidently regarded as a reliable technique for reversing or killing cancer.

And yet, it seems, from research studies and success stories, that the Ketogenic Diet does just that!

Evidence to Support the Keto Diet as the Best Option When Cancer is Already Present in Your Dog

In 2002, a study from the Animal Cancer Center and Colorado State University sought to connect the dots between nutrition and cancer.

The study still serves as one of the most recent and well-conducted insights into nutritional therapy as cancer treatment.

Although the tests specifically did not relate to Keto, or diet as an all-around cancer cure, it did discuss cases where nutrition is specifically essential in fighting the effects of cancer.

The reports themselves do not confirm that the Ketogenic Diet is a cancer cure, as they were not seeking to prove the efficiency of Keto, to begin with. However, the collected results are very conclusive that diet can serve to be pivotal in the assistance of eliminating cancer. The study also showed that minimizing carbohydrates in the diet provides considerable nutritional support toward healing the body.

This study, in particular, looked into one of the most alarming and widely occurring side effects of cancer: weight loss. Cancer cachexia can create any number of results, and there are currently not any simple solutions for this condition.

In addition to being a treatment for cancer cachexia, fast weight loss, the study found that nutritional therapy is important to minimize the harmful impacts that mainstream forms of cancer treatment can have on the body.

The study further emphasizes the time sensitivity in taking control of a patient's diet. The sooner a low carb diet is introduced and managed the faster the patient can begin to reap its benefits.

The study sought to test how the level of carbohydrate intake in a dog suffering from cancer would influence their health.

This hypothesis was tested by splitting a group of dogs, which suffered from lymphoma into two separate groups. One of the groups was given a diet rich in a high content of carbohydrates. The second group was fed a diet with a high fat content.

Unsurprisingly, the animals that were fed a diet of a high fat content experienced better results.

These dogs were more likely to be cleared of cancer, which shows that a low carb diet was a beneficial treatment to eradicate cancer.

Through all the research conducted in this study, it was concluded that a diet with limited carbohydrates and a moderate amount of proteins, fiber, and fatty acids would be most advisable to a dog suffering from the effects of cancer.

This is exactly what the Ketogenic Diet is.

While the study specifically hadn't sought to prove the legitimacy of Keto, in exploring the connection between diet and cancer's side effects, they had unwittingly confirmed the Ketogenic Diet works as a cancer cure.

In 2011, Rainer Klement and Ulrike Kämmerer, combined several scientific elements including Warburg's hypothesis, to determine whether limiting carbohydrates could actually serve to prevent or halt cancer and its effects.

Like the Colorado State University's study, these researchers were also not aimed at proving the efficiency of a Ketogenic Diet specifically. But, by looking into the effects of carbohydrate levels in a cancer patient they were also able to support that the Ketogenic Diet works.

The study looked at the connection between genetic mutation and diet as a reason cancer exists. In researching through the decades, they noted the rise of modern diseases in correlation to our modern diet's high sugar content. The study goes on to explain cancer's preference of glucose in place of any other energy source.

Hello again, Mr. Warbug!

Through glycolysis, cancer cells can continue to mutate within the body. The study proved that the preferred energy source of cancerous cells over any other was - yep, you guessed it, glucose! Or sugar.

This research and countless other studies now render it obvious that carbohydrates benefit cancer cell growth and production. Period.

Another study found the mice, with a more than fifty-percent genetic risk for developing cancer, were able to remain cancer-free for an entire year when switched to a low-carbohydrate diet.

The mice that remained on a regular diet did not experience the same results, nearly half of that group developed tumors. More than half!

Study after study that we've researched involving people, mice and canines, conclusions time and time again, that ultimately, a diet low in carbohydrate intake could have a strong likelihood of decreasing cancer risks.

The studies also assure that the diet is safe in patients and has not shown any harmful effects.

Half of these studies went on to say that the negative effects of cancer on the body's metabolism could be counteracted by a low carbohydrate diet such as Keto.

It is well-known through these studies, that calorie restriction of carbohydrates, in the face of cancer, can be lifesaving.

Through a keto-based diet, the body can mirror these effects and reap similar benefits that happen during the fasting poses, without the often-times devastating effects of that stressful process - especially on a weakened body.

CHAPTER 14:
How to Talk Keto With Your Vet

Why Talking with Your Vet About the Keto Diet Might Fill You with Doubt and How To Overcome It

Your veterinarian might not know anything about the Ketogenic Diet, and that could be frustrating for you. Especially if your dog has a cancer diagnosis and you're reading this guide, then asking your vet for a professional option on the topic.

Simply know that people don't know what they don't know.

Your vet might be part of the old-school thinking, even if biologically in age he or she is young. That old-school way of thinking, in the medical community, is that nutrition does not play a role in the health of the body - whether human or canine.

While it's frustrating, it should also make you stop and think about what you believe. What your vet believes to be true matters, yes, but not at the cost of your dog's health.

Do you believe what your four-legged friend eats is important? If you do, then you may wish to seek the advice of another veterinarian. One who is up-to-date with new ways of thinking and sees the entire body from cellular level to furry coat, as a cohesive being, which is supported, or harmed, by the food he or she eats.

If you don't believe the what you canine eats is important and has an impact on your doggy's health, then this guide is probably not for you.

Please keep reading, as it may just open your eyes, but know too that we aren't selling anything here. We are educating. We are dog lovers who care. We have found the science-based research that proves cancer cells feed on sugar or glucose and thrive. We have discovered the research, again science-based, that shows the cancer cells within human bodies and doggy bodies alike being paused, minimized and, in some cases, disappearing altogether.

Read this guide cover to cover. Do some research of your own. Check out Ketogenic websites; you'll find a listing in the *Additional Resources* section of this guide. Remember, knowledge is power.

Arm yourself today because your furriest family member's life may just depend on it. And you.

CHAPTER 15:
Guide to Keto In Humans

Want to Go Keto with Your Canine Bestie?

It might just be the healthiest choice you can make for both of you.

It only takes a few minutes of research after typing Ketogenic Diet into the Google research bar, to see you've stumbled upon a winner of success stories with life-changing impact.

One such story is of a man struggling with cancer who credits shifting his dietary habits to Keto with saving his own his life.

Dr. Fred Hatfield had a seemingly picture-perfect life, was in excellent health. His claim-to-fame was as "Dr. Squat" as he became known as one of the first people to squat over a hundred pounds.

Well, his world collapsed under a heavy weight when in 2012, he was diagnosed with metastatic cancer and given, an estimated, three months to live by several prestigious doctors.

Not yet ready to admit defeat, Hatfield turned to metabolic therapy as another form of treatment. Dr. Squat, as we will affectionately call him, cut out carbohydrates and managed to starve the cancer cells within his skeletal structure.

Did you catch that? From three months to live to cancer-free.

A Beginner's Guide to Keto For the Two-Legged You

Keto, or the Ketogenic Diet - well known for being low in carbohydrates, is a state in which the body produces ketones in the liver, which are then used for energy.

The Ketogenic Diet is also known as a low carb high fat (LCHF) that limits carbohydrates typically lower than 30 grams per day.

What Is The Keto Diet For Humans?

When you're on the keto diet, because it's lower in carbohydrates, most of your calories come from fats and protein to fuel the body.

When you ingest carbohydrates, your body breaks them down into the simplest molecule possible, glucose. This molecule forces your body to produce insulin. Insulin transports carbs across membranes to either be used directly as energy or to be stored for later use (either in fat or muscle/liver glycogen).

Glucose is the easiest molecule for your body to convert into and use for energy at any given time. Glucose will be the first thing chosen, by the body, to use as an energy source.

Insulin is produced to process the glucose in your bloodstream, to transport it around your body, and to store it where necessary. When your body is using glycogen or glucose as its main energy source, your body will not need to burn fat.

Are you having an AH-HA Moment?!

It's, therefore, more likely that your body will store fat so it can be used at a later point in time when your energy (glycogen) levels are low. So, when you're on a higher carbohydrate diet, your body will use glycogen as its main energy source.

Changing Things Up By Entering Ketosis

However, when you lower your carb intake, your body is pushed into ketosis. Keto is a natural process which we rely on when our food intake is low for an extended period. As a human race, before more civilized times, when we had to hunt for our food, keto was the norm for our bodies.

The Keto state helps us continue to thrive.

While in ketosis, your body produces ketones from breaking down fats in your liver. This is how your body continues to produce energy to fuel your body's demands.

The ultimate goal of adopting a Keto Diet is forcing your body into this metabolic state in which it produces ketones. You might think you are, but YOU ARE NOT STARVING YOUR BODY.

You are simply limiting your body's consumption of carbohydrates and replacing it with dietary fats and proteins. Our bodies have evolved to be able to perform normal daily functions without carbohydrates. When we saturate our body with fats and proteins, they burn ketones as their main energy source.

What Happens to My Body During Keto?

Due to the North American diet, most people typically consume high quantities of carbohydrates on a daily basis.

Our bodies are used to this routine of breaking down carbohydrates, into glucose, to then use that for energy.

However, our bodies have only a few enzymes to deal with fats. If we don't need them, our body stops making them. And when we are living of carbs (glucose as fuel) and not burning fat, guess what? We stop producing these fat burning enzymes.

Instead, fats are stored for energy. The constant buildup of fats stored for energy is what leads to fat gain and, eventually, obesity.

We are not meant to store fats as we do. We are not meant to eat carbs as we do. We are not meant to be so unhealthy, so overweight and suffering from so many diseases.

So once the body encounters a lack of glycogen on the Ketogenic Diet, a lower consumption of carbohydrates to break down into glucose, and an increase in fat intake, the body adjusts by building up a new supply of these enzymes.

As your body begins to enter a ketogenic state, it will use the glycogen that is left. Eventually, your muscles and liver will be depleted of glycogen.

This is a good thing and the first phase in the Keto process.

However, this depletion can lead to a lack of energy, a lethargic feeling, dizziness, headaches, and sometimes even "flu-like" symptoms. And that's normal.

You Could Experience Possible Flu-Like Symptoms When Starting Ketogenic Diet

It's not entirely clear what exactly causes these feelings, but it's believed to be the lack of electrolytes (which are flushed out of the body).

Carbohydrates help bring fluid to your muscles, and the ratio of water to carbohydrates is roughly 4:1 (in grams). This is similar to the diuretic effect and explains why, when athletes want to drop to the weight class below where they currently are - say in bodybuilding or wrestling, they decrease their carbohydrate consumption. The decrease in carb consumption lowers their fluid retention and therefore their weight.

However, during a Ketogenic Diet, it's advisable to make your water and sodium intakes higher than normal, to prevent these feelings and to make your first experience of ketosis more enjoyable. And seriously, water is a great filler and a natural way to detox.

Remember, toxins live in the fatty tissue. When you enter a state of ketosis or when you drop the carbohydrate intake, your energy must now come from somewhere else - your fat storage. Whoopie!

Well, yes, but also, watch out. Your bloodstream will be flooded with toxins that have been stored in your fat storage. And this is normal. And another possible reason for those flu-like symptoms.

A typical person who starts a Ketogenic Diet and consumes 20-40 grams of net carbs per day takes approximately two weeks to enter Keto. If net carbs are dropped to fewer than 15 grams of carbohydrates, the adaption process can be shortened to approximately seven to ten days.

The more physical activity you participate in also plays a role. Lifting and performing sprints decreases the adaptation time because your body burns glycogen to fuel those intensive activities. Some people report a loss of strength or endurance during this phase and once they've entered ketosis. This is completely normal.

Once you have adapted to this state and your body has become more efficient at using fats for fuel, your performance will begin to rise back to baseline. Many also report that they seem to have more energy throughout the day and are more focused once they have adapted to this Ketogenic State. I don't know about you, but I like the sound of that.

CHAPTER 16:
Comparing Keto in Dogs & Humans

Does My Dog Experience The Same Thing I Do On the Ketogenic Diet?

We can only guess what our four-legged friends experience while on the Ketogenic Diet.

Based on studies, science, the way cells work and the structure of the human and doggy body, the chances are that, yes, they experience similar things.

That fact that the Ketogenic Diet changes the focus from glucose energy to ketone energy is the same in humans as it is in dogs suggests that your canine might experience a week or two of not feeling great. Or your pup might be full of energy. We are each so unique and really can't give a blanket statement about what our dogs will experience.

Just like my experience going Keto maybe be very different from yours.

All you can do is observe and be there for your dog with love, support and the facts found in this guide to back you up every step of the way.

Remember, your pup can't share when in pain, but there may be signs of not being hungry, not wanting to do much of anything, and weight loss.

Take each symptom in stride and stay in touch with a veterinarian you trust who understands the connecting between health, healing, and nutrition - if not the Ketogenic Diet specifically.

Three Basics To Remember As Your Canine Starts On the Ketogenic Diet

1. **A skipped meal or two is not too big of a concern as your dog will eat when hungry.**

Should you doggy skip three meals in a row, try offering beef broth (recipe in the back of this guide) or 1/2 cup of goat's milk. Both are super high in nutrients.

If those options do not work, consult your vet.

2. If your four-legged friend doesn't want to play fetch the first week, don't be discouraged.

That little body is undergoing a strenuous workout under all the fur as the process of shifting from glucose consumption to fat consumption is taking place.

3. Your bestie needs love, comfort, and support more than anything else.

Be present as much as possible. And keep a journal of all your canine's reactions, feedings, test scores and activities so that if you need to contact your veterinarian or see the improvement, by looking backward, you will have it at your fingertips.

CHAPTER 17:
More Success Stories

Success Stories

There are amazing successes happening every day with the Ketogenic Diet for canines.

You will find new sites popping up now that you are on the Keto path and you will have access to more and more good news as the days, weeks, months and years go by. We hope that YOUR furry family member's story will be here next. That you and your canine family take hold of this amazing opportunity called *The Cancer Cure Diet for Dogs*, and you run with it - all the way to a cure, for your cancer diagnosed four-legged friend. OR all the way to maintaining and reaching the highest standard of health for your bestie.

See, we care. We bring you these stories (and we hope you share yours soon by emailing us at dogingtonpost@gmail.com) because facts tell but stories sell. These stories will keep you going when you get frustrated with the math of the Ketogenic Diet - and you just might. And it's okay.

These stories will keep you motivated to keep Keto happening for your bestie even when life gets super busy, or something comes up.

Dax's Story

Aliments: Seizures, Allergies, Anxiety, Itchy Skin, Inflammation
Time the Ketogenic Diet: 1.5 years
7-year-old German Shepard/Coon Hound Mix

We have owned Dax for five years. He is a rescue. When we got him, he was in bad shape. His previous owners had beaten him and used a shock collar on him.

He used to cry in his sleep and had terrible anxiety. He also suffered from seizures.

We tried many different treatments, creams, and foods and he would be "OK" for a while, but then it would stop working, and he would revert. We would hold him through his seizures while he cried. It was heartbreaking.

16 months ago, I embarked on a keto diet. Shortly after I began, I started looking into putting Dax on it. Within a few weeks, he showed massive differences.

He didn't cry, his skin looked better, he started jumping around like he must of as a puppy. He also started playing.

The vet was very surprised. He hasn't had a seizure, his skin has cleared up, and no more allergies or inflammation. It is quite remarkable. We were so impressed with his changes, we changed our other dog to Keto right away. Keto is fantastic for both of them.

https://ketogenic.com/pawsandclaws/dax/

Marshall's Story

Aliments: Inflammatory Bowel Disease, Meningitis, Auto-Immune Disease
Time the Ketogenic Diet: 2 years

I have been feeding my 6yr old dog (Marshall) commercial raw dog food for 2 years.

Primal Pet Foods and Steve's Real Food brands consisting of turkey & sardine and beef respectively. They average between 2% to 3% carbs.

Initially my dog presented with allergy symptoms before the age of 1 while on kibble. I tried grain free, homemade cooked, and homemade raw; none of these worked long term.

His allergy turned into IBD and after 4 years of trial and error I found out it was all about the carbs/starch in his diet.

After starting him on the Primal and Steve's his IBD became manageable, no more vomiting or acid reflux.

https://ketogenic.com/pawsandclaws/marshall/

Alex's Story

From Terminal To Healthy

Alex is a 90-pound pit bull/American Staffordshire terrier mix that is 10 years old (2013). He was diagnosed with osteosarcoma that had not yet metastasized. His vet informed him the options were amputation, chemo, and radiation.

The dog was in pain and had a severe limp, barely putting weight on that leg. The owner switched Alex to an all raw food diet, removed all the sugar and carbs out of the diet…Within three months the tumor was hardly noticeable.

The bump left is scar tissues in the exact spot where the biopsy was taken. May 2015, 1 1/2 years later the dog is happy and running around like nothing ever happened.

He was initially given 2-3 months to live if not having the leg amputated, chemo, and radiation. Bone cancer can be very stubborn and slow to heal, in this case, it happened rather fast.

https://longlivingpets.com/cancer-and-pets/testimonials

Teddy's Amazing Story

A 5-year-old golden retriever/lab was diagnosed with an aggressive cancer.

Sarah, the owner, eliminated all sugars and switched to an all raw food diet. Along with apricot added to the diet in a specific format, which is a healing agent, the fast-spreading cancer took a turn.

After just 2 days the tumor is no longer red and infected. It's now pink and the infection is reduced and almost gone.

Five days into the treatment Teddy is healing nicely. No limping anymore and he eats and acts normal again.

28 days. The tumor is down over 70%.

TruDog Success Stories:

A Boston Terrier's Cancerous Lumps - Disappeared!

I originally ordered the Boost Me on a promotion. I figured if my dog doesn't like it, I won't be out a lot of money. I also ordered because I read the info about this product. My Boston Terrier had these fairly large growths on her neck and side. The vet told me that they had cancerous cells in them and wanted me to have them removed. Long story short, the growth on her neck completely disappeared within a month of feeding her Boost Me, Feed Me, and Treat Me. I only added these in addition to her regular food. I scheduled surgery to have the tumor on her side removed. About a month after the first growth disappeared, the other one went down dramatically. I cancelled the surgery and opted to keep a eye on it. I can't say 100% that it was your foods and treats that did it, but that's the only thing I changed in her routine. In my opinion, I feel that they have helped her in a big way. At 9 years old, lately she has more pep and energy than ever before. Sometimes she even acts like a puppy. Both her and my other dog love it. They chow down on their food now like it's the greatest thing in the world. If my dogs love to eat their food with Boost Me, along with your other products, and they positively benefit my babies, then I'm sold!

- Arlene L.

Bailey's Story

This story is about Bailey, my wife Fama and myself's furry little friend. Bailey is a miniature schnauzer that we purchased eight years ago from one of our local pet stores. After a few days Bailey began to have a problem. He was having diarrhea with blood in it. After changing foods several times with no change we took him to our vet who referred us to another vet, who referred us to another vet, until we finally ended up at a vet's office who's specialty was diagnosing pets with problems. He performed a test similar to a colonoscopy, and discovered he had colitis. He then told us that there was no cure, but it was manageable with the proper diet and medications. He prescribed prednisone, amoxicillin, & Canine I.D. which he forwarded to our vet for filling. Little did we know that the prednisone was supposed to end after two weeks and the rest continue from that point forward. Our vet continued the prednisone along with the food and amoxicillin for the next seven years. About a year ago Bailey began having severe diarrhea, bleeding, and was losing weight as well. After many trips to our vet trying

several different antibiotics and other meds, we ended up where we started, at the diagnosing vet's office. When we showed him all the meds we were giving him is when he noticed that we were still giving him the prednisone. That's when he about died, he said we had to wean Bailey off the prednisone. We couldn't stop it cold turkey, and he had to give him some of the most powerful drugs there was to try and get him well. That's when things really got tough for Bailey, my wife and myself. We were in the middle of many sleepless nights trying to keep our thoughts positive. When we had to take Bailey back to the diagnosis vet, he told us that he thought that Bailey had cancer, which we were very familiar with since we had already had to put two other furry friends down in past years. We were at the end of our rope, didn't want to go through this again. We called on our church going friends and asked them to put Bailey on their prayer list. We asked all our family members to pray for Bailey, and my wife and myself prayed earnestly for Bailey to be cured from this terrible disease. One night I was sitting in front of my computer just looking for anything that might help cure Bailey of his problem when an infomercial came up on my screen. It was about a thirty minute infomercial about TruDog. I watched and listened to every minute of it. When it was over I told my wife that God just sent me a message through the TruDog infomercial. We immediately ordered some of the food on the TruDog website. Bailey was weaned off the prednisone by the time we got the food. We started feeding him the food immediately, and by the way he loved it. We know that God has a plan for everyone and everything and I am truly convinced that God sent that infomercial to me through TruDog, and that all the prayers that were prayed for Bailey were answered. Bailey is a happy healthy little furry friend who is completely healed of colitis. He has gained all his weight back, has normal bowel movements with no bleeding, and all of us are getting a good night's sleep thanks to God and TruDog.
THANK YOU LORI FOR ALL YOU DO FOR SO MANY FOLKS OUT THERE WHO HAVE FURRY FRIENDS ENJOYING GOOD HEALTHY LIVES FROM THE DEDICATION AND SACRIFICE YOU HAVE PUT INTO A PRODUCT THAT WE TRUST.

Thank You,
Eddie Grigg

CHAPTER 18:
Bonus Recipes

Bone Broth Recipe

A perfect addition to your Keto-dog's diet, bone broth is as delicious as it is nutrient-dense.

Packed with amino acids, vitamins, and minerals, when used as a supplement to your dog's diet, bone broth -
• promotes a healthy digestive system
• detoxifies the liver
• promotes healthy joint function
• encourages picky, sick, or elderly dogs to eat.

This homemade bone broth recipe is slow-cooked over low heat, increasing nutrient density and bioavailability.

You'll need:
• Large Crockpot/Slow Cooker
• Bones - cooked or raw, organic & grass-fed whenever possible
  *Our favorite bones for broth include: marrow bones, joint bones (with cartilage), duck/turkey necks, chicken frames, and even chicken feet - but ANY bones will do!
• Raw Apple Cider Vinegar - 1 tablespoon per gallon
• Optional Add-Ins: Fresh herbs or veggies (kale, kelp, medicinal mushrooms, broccoli, parsley, oregano, turmeric, etc)

1. Fill large crockpot with bones.
2. Add water to pot until bones are completely covered, plus an additional 2-3 inches of water.
3. Add raw apple cider vinegar to the pot.
4. Turn crockpot on to HIGH for 1 hour, then reduce heat to LOW and let simmer for 24-hours.
5. Strain out all bones and meat, leaving only broth in the pot.
6. Add optional ingredients (herbs, vegetables, turmeric, etc) to the broth.
7. Turn off heat and let broth cool completely, then refrigerate for 2 to 3 hours. After refrigeration, your bone broth may develop a thin layer of white fat on top. Just break the fat "crust" apart and discard. Bone broth below the fat layer will have a jelly-like consistency.
8. Spoon out and serve as needed.

Feel free to experiment with different types of bones - you can even toss in bones leftover from your own meals - and healthy, dog-safe herbs and vegetables each time you cook up a new batch.

Broth can be kept in refrigerator for up to 5 days or can be frozen for several months.

Remove Stains & Eliminate Odors Naturally

Vinegar-Baking Soda Spray is simple, inexpensive, and works on blood and urine stains in particular, plus gets rid of odors. White vinegar is a miraculous substance that will get rid of even old accident stains. Baking soda is nature's odor remover.

Ingredients
- 2 cups white distilled vinegar
- 2 cups of lukewarm water
- 4 generous tablespoons of baking soda
- Spray bottle (optional)

For Use on a Fresh Stain
Thoroughly blot up as much of whatever it is you're cleaning up. Take time doing this step as you need to absorb all the liquid that is on the carpet or sofa cushion. Fold a rag and blot, then a fresh rag and stand on it!

1. Mix 2 cups of white distilled vinegar with 2 cups of lukewarm water in a large bowl.
2. Add 4 heaping tablespoons of baking soda, adding it in smaller amounts if it threatens to fizz over.
3. Pour into a spray bottle and thoroughly spray the area.
4. Let sit for 5 minutes, then gently rub and blot up with a soft cloth.

You can also simply pour some straight from the bowl over the stain if you don't have a spray bottle.

For Heavy Duty Stains or Major Odors on Rugs or Carpets
1. Instead of adding the baking soda to the liquid, sprinkle the dry powder over the area where the accident occurred.
2. Let it break down and deodorize for about 5 minutes, then vacuum.

3. Apply the water/vinegar solution as in the first set of directions.

Have a Nasty, Smelly Stain? Try this:
1. Mix up your water and vinegar solution.
2. After blotting up any excess fluid, sprinkle a generous amount of the dry baking soda over the soiled area.
3. Pour the water and vinegar solution directly onto the baking soda to create a mini cleaning volcano that will fizz - cool to do with kids! - that will actively eat away at the stain.
4. Blot and rub gently dry with a soft cloth after letting it sit for 5 minutes.

Chemical Free Doggy Shampoo
(Note: If you have cats in the house, many essential oils are toxic to them. Only use this shampoo on your canine friends)

Ingredients
- 350 ml purified or distilled water (not tap)
- 1 tbsp Castile soap
- 2 drops of lavender essential oil
- 2 drops peppermint essential oil
- 2 drops eucalyptus essential oil
- 2 drops rosemary essential oil
- Bottle (a large1.5 litter water bottle works well)

Mix all ingredients together in a jar before pouring into a bottle.
Shake the bottle each time you use the shampoo.
Lather your dog well when bathing and rinse thoroughly.

Note: If you have a dog with skin sensitivity, consider doing a test first on one paw/leg and chest area and or the spine of your canine going back toward the tail.

Doggy Deodorant, No Kidding!
(Note: If you have cats in the house, many essential oils are toxic to them. Only use this deodorant on your canine friends)

Ingredients
- Spray bottle

- 10 drops lavender essential oil
- 6 drops orange oil
- 6 drops peppermint essential oil
- 3 drops eucalyptus essential oil
- 8 ounces of purified or distilled water

Directions
1. Mix all the ingredients into the spray bottle and shake well.
2. Cover the face and eyes of your dog and spray on their coat until it's as if they walked for a moment in a light mist.
3. Allow to dry.

Note: For dogs with allergies or skin issues, test a small area first, and never spray on wounds, rashes or infected areas.

Basic Everyday Floor Cleaner For All Floor Types

This is the perfect everyday cleaner for your sealed wood, tile, laminate and linoleum. And it's simple, healthy and inexpensive. Your pets will thank you with fewer allergies and more energy!

Simply mix equal parts of white vinegar and hot water, and mop. There's no need to rinse, and the vinegar smell dissipates once the floors have dried. Cool, right?! Plus, the vinegar acts as a mild disinfectant and leaves a nice shine.

Note on water: If you have hard water or live in an area where chlorine is used in the pipes to bring the water to your location, consider using distilled water.

Note on essential oils: If you have felines in the home, please take note as some essential oils are NOT healthy for them. Do a bit of research to make sure what you use is also cat-friendly.

Additional Resources

The Dogington Post
www.DogingtonPost.com

The KetoPet Sanctuary
www.ketopetsanctuary.com

Keep the Tail Wagging
www.keepthetailwagging.com

The Ketovangelist
www.ketovangelist.com

Completely Keto
www.completelyketo.com

Further Reading

Keto for Cancer
Ketogenic Metabolic Therapy as a Targeted Nutritional Strategy
Miriam Kalamian, EdM, MS, CNS

Pointing the Bone at Cancer
Dr. Ian Billinghurst, B.V.Sc., Hons

Keto Meal Plan Worksheet for _____ Date _____

Dog's Weight	_____ pounds
1 5 9 Too Thin Ideal Obese Body Condition Score (circle one)	1 2 3 4 5 6 7 8 9
Ex: 15 calories/pound 20 calories/pound Recommended Calories Per Pound (based on activity level and body condition score)	_____ calories/pound
_____ x _____ = weight calories/pound Total Daily Caloric Intake (over two meals)	_____ calories/day
Chosen Ketogenic Ratio (based on dog's specific needs)	0.5:1 1:1 2:1 3:1 4:1 (circle one)

Fill in the **Nutrition Informaion Chart** below based on 1 gram each of your preferred meat, oil (fat) and veggies:

Food	Amount (grams)	Fat (grams)	Protein (grams)	Carb (grams)	Fiber (grams)	Net Carbs (grams)	Cals (kCal)	Cals from Fat
Meat:	1.00							
Oil:	1.00							
Veg:	1.00							

*NOTE: Carbs - Fiber = Net Carbs

Determine How Many Vegetables to Serve Each Day:

_____ x   0.2 grams veggies
dog's weight   for 15cal/lb
0.27 grams veggies
for 20cal/lb   = [_____]   x 2 meals/day = _____
grams of veggies   **grams of veggies**
per meal   **per day**

_____ x _____ = _____
grams of veggies   calories per   calories from
per day   1-gram of veg   vegetables
(refer to Nutrition Information Chart)

Determine How Much Meat to Serve Each Day:

_____ x _____ = _____ - _____ = _____
recommended   varies depending   daily calories   calories from   daily calories
daily calories   on Keto Ratio   from meat & veg   vegetables   from meat

Keto Ratio	Multiply By:
0.5:1	.50
1:1	.50
2:1	.33
3:1	.25
4:1	.20

_____ ÷ _____ = [_____]
daily calories   calories per   grams of meat
from meat   1-gram meat   per meal
(refer to Nutrition Information Chart)

_____
x 2 meals/day =   **grams of meat**
per day

Determine Value of PROTEINgrams + CARBgrams (per meal):

$$\boxed{} \text{x} \; \frac{\text{net carbs per}}{\text{1-gram of veggies}} \; = \; \text{CARBgrams}$$

grams of veggies
per meal

(refer to Nutrition Information Chart)

$$\boxed{} \text{x} \; \frac{\text{grams protein per}}{\text{1-gram of meat}} \; = \; \text{PROTEINgrams}$$

grams of meat
per meal

(refer to Nutrition Information Chart)

CARBgrams _____

+

PROTEINgrams _____

=

PROTEINgrams
+CARBgrams _____

Use The Ketogenic Ratio Formula to Determine FATgrams: (FATgrams to PROTEINgrams+CARBgrams)

Keto Ratio	Use:
0.5:1	.5
1:1	1
2:1	2
3:1	3
4:1	4

$$\frac{}{\substack{\text{varies depending} \\ \text{on keto ratio}}} \; \text{x} \; \frac{}{\substack{\text{PROTEINgrams+} \\ \text{CARBgrams}}} \; = \; \text{FATgrams}$$

Determine How Much Oil (Fat) to Add Each Day:

$$\boxed{} \text{x} \; \frac{\text{grams of fat per}}{\text{1-gram of meat}} \; = \; \boxed{}$$

grams of meat
per meal

FATgrams from
meat

(refer to Nutrition Information Chart)

$$\frac{}{\text{FATgrams}} \; - \; \boxed{\substack{\text{FATgrams from} \\ \text{meat}}} \; = \; \frac{}{\substack{\text{FATgrams} \\ \text{still needed}}}$$

$$\frac{}{\substack{\text{FATgrams} \\ \text{still needed}}} \; \div \; \frac{}{\substack{\text{grams of fat per} \\ \text{1-gram of oil}}} \; = \; \frac{}{\substack{\text{grams of oil} \\ \text{per meal}}} \; \text{x 2 meals/day} = \boxed{\substack{\text{_____} \\ \textbf{grams of oil} \\ \textbf{per day}}}$$

(refer to Nutrition Information Chart)

Keto Meal Plan Worksheet for _____ Date _____

Dog's Weight	_____ pounds
1 **5** **9** Too Thin Ideal Obese Body Condition Score (circle one)	1 2 3 4 5 6 7 8 9
Ex: 15 calories/pound 20 calories/pound **Recommended Calories Per Pound** (based on activity level and body condition score)	_____ calories/pound
_____ X _____ = weight calories/pound **Total Daily Caloric Intake** (over two meals)	_____ calories/day
Chosen Ketogenic Ratio (based on dog's specific needs)	0.5:1 1:1 2:1 3:1 4:1 (circle one)

Fill in the **Nutrition Informaion Chart** below based on 1 gram each of your preferred meat, oil (fat) and veggies:

Food	Amount (grams)	Fat (grams)	Protein (grams)	Carb (grams)	Fiber (grams)	Net Carbs (grams)	Cals (kCal)	Cals from Fat
Meat:	1.00							
Oil:	1.00							
Veg:	1.00							

*NOTE: Carbs - Fiber = Net Carbs

Determine How Many Vegetables to Serve Each Day:

_____ X   0.2 grams veggies   = ┌──────────┐ x 2 meals/day = _____
dog's weight   for 15cal/lb   grams of veggies   **grams of veggies**
     0.27 grams veggies   per meal   **per day**
     for 20cal/lb

_____ X _____ = _____
grams of veggies   calories per   calories from
per day   1-gram of veg   vegetables
    (refer to Nutrition Information Chart)

Determine How Much Meat to Serve Each Day:

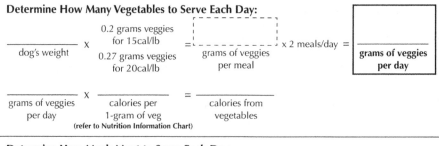

_____ X _____ = _____ - _____ = _____
recommended   varies depending   daily calories   calories from   daily calories
daily calories   on Keto Ratio   from meat & veg   vegetables   from meat

Keto Ratio	Multiply By:
0.5:1	.50
1:1	.50
2:1	.33
3:1	.25
4:1	.20

_____ ÷ _____ = ┌──────────┐
daily calories   calories per   grams of meat
from meat   1-gram meat   per meal
   (refer to Nutrition Information Chart)

x 2 meals/day = _____
**grams of meat
per day**

Determine Value of PROTEINgrams + CARBgrams (per meal):

$$\boxed{} \times \frac{\text{net carbs per}}{\text{1-gram of veggies}} = \underline{\qquad}$$

grams of veggies   net carbs per   CARBgrams
per meal   1-gram of veggies
(refer to Nutrition Information Chart)

CARBgrams _____

+

PROTEINgrams _____

=

$$\boxed{} \times \frac{\text{grams protein per}}{\text{1-gram of meat}} = \underline{\qquad}$$

grams of meat   grams protein per   PROTEINgrams
per meal   1-gram of meat
(refer to Nutrition Information Chart)

PROTEINgrams
+CARBgrams _____

Use The Ketogenic Ratio Formula to Determine FATgrams: (FATgrams to PROTEINgrams+CARBgrams)

Keto Ratio	Use:
0.5:1	.5
1:1	1
2:1	2
3:1	3
4:1	4

$$\frac{\text{varies depending}}{\text{on keto ratio}} \times \frac{\text{PROTEINgrams+}}{\text{CARBgrams}} = \frac{}{\text{FATgrams}}$$

Determine How Much Oil (Fat) to Add Each Day:

$$\boxed{} \times \frac{\text{grams of fat per}}{\text{1-gram of meat}} = \boxed{}$$

grams of meat   grams of fat per   FATgrams from
per meal   1-gram of meat   meat
(refer to Nutrition Information Chart)

$$\frac{}{\text{FATgrams}} - \frac{\boxed{}}{\text{FATgrams from meat}} = \frac{}{\text{FATgrams still needed}}$$

$$\frac{}{\substack{\text{FATgrams} \\ \text{still needed}}} \div \frac{\text{grams of fat per}}{\text{1-gram of oil}} = \frac{}{\substack{\text{grams of oil} \\ \text{per meal}}} \times 2\ \text{meals/day} = \boxed{\substack{\textbf{grams of oil} \\ \textbf{per day}}}$$

(refer to Nutrition Information Chart)

Made in the USA
Coppell, TX
07 January 2022